DISCOVERING HISTORY

THE ERA OF THE
SECOND WORLD WAR

TONY & STEVE LANCASTER
with LISA FABRY

Series Editors
NEIL TONGE &
PETER HEPPLEWHITE

CPL

Causeway Press Ltd

To Jane, Lisa, Ruth and Sarah

Acknowledgement

Many thanks to Lisa Fabry, especially for her work on Chapter 8. Thanks also to Mike Haralambos for all his help and support.

Tony and Steve Lancaster
March, 1993

Note to teachers

1. **The Focus pages**

   Each chapter contains a Focus page which aims to engage the reader, excite curiosity and raise issues. All Focus pages are based on primary source material.

2. **The Sources**

   Most of the written sources are taken either from original documents or from the writings of historians. In some cases the language has been adapted to aid comprehension.

   Statistical data needs to be treated with caution. There is often considerable variation between statistics drawn from standard works. An example of this variation is given in Source E, page 61.

3. **The Teachers' Guide**

   A teachers' guide is available. It is photocopiable and provides assessment tests, guidance for marking, additional information and worksheets with further activities.

CONTENTS

1 INTRODUCTION

When the First World War of 1914-18 was over, people began to describe it as the 'Great War' or the 'war to end all wars'. It had lasted for just over four years and had cost over 8 million lives. When the war was over people hoped that nothing like it would ever happen again.

Although it is called a 'world war', it was mainly fought in Europe. In 1914 the armies of Germany and Austria-Hungary (the Central Powers) invaded Belgium and northern France in the west and Russia in the east. They were met by the armies of the Allies (Britain, France, Italy and Russia). The result was a stalemate (neither side could advance). Each side dug trenches and then tried to capture the trenches opposite. When one side charged, the other side used machine guns to shoot them down. Thousands died for the sake of advancing a few yards.

The turning point came in 1917 when the USA joined the war on the side of the Allies. The extra resources brought by the Americans were sufficient for the Allies to defeat the Central Powers.

Source A World War I - participants and casualties

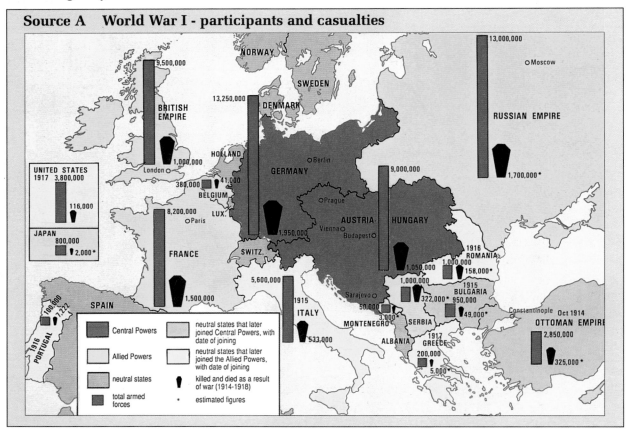

Source B Trench warfare

We went over. We hadn't got half way when Jerry (the Germans) started machine gunning. If a bullet hit us, that was it. I'd have been blown to smithereens. I heard Tommy Winkler go 'Ah'. He was my mate - and he was gone - just like that. I got to within 20 yards of the German trench and heard someone shout, 'Retreat! Back to the trenches.' I looked around and there was nobody there! I crawled back on my hands and knees and got back in our trench. There was nobody left alive.

W.H. Nixon recalling the battle of Loos in 1915

Source C New methods of warfare

A tank crossing a German trench, painted in 1917

In the 19th century most wars were decided by 'set-piece' battles – the cavalry (soldiers on horseback) would charge and the infantry follow on foot with rifles and cannons. By 1914, however, industrialisation had brought great changes. New weapons (such as machine guns and mustard gas) caused enormous loss of life. Trains and lorries were used to transport troops. Aircraft fought battles in the air and submarines attacked steel warships at sea. During the war a new weapon – the tank – was developed by the Allies. The tanks used in the First World War had a maximum speed of 5 mph and often broke down or got bogged down.

Source D

On 9 November 1918 (the day on which Germany agreed to surrender) Germany collapsed like a house of cards. All that we had lived for, all that we had bled four long years to keep, was gone. We no longer had a native land of which we might be proud. Order vanished. All authority disappeared. Chaos.

General Ludendorff (a German commander in the First World War), 'My War Memories', 1933

Source E

My dearest Mum and Dad and all,

Hurrah for our side! Can you believe the war is over? I'm sure I can't. It seems too wonderful to believe, yet here there is no excitement, no celebrations and everything is going on in the same old way. The army has taken the happenings of the past few weeks in a calm and subdued manner. Not even a cheer was raised when first we heard the official news. But deep down there is the knowledge that soon we shall be seeing home and that is what the signing of the Armistice (agreement to end fighting) means to us. It means home.

Your ever loving boy,

Bert

B.O. Stokes, letter written from France, 18 November 1918

Activities

1. What does Source A tell us about the extent and effect of the First World War? Explain your answer.

2. Using Sources A and B explain why the war was later described as 'the war to end all wars'.

3. Look at Sources B and C.
   a) How did the First World War differ from previous wars?
   b) What advantages did the invention of tanks bring?

4. Using Sources D and E describe how different people reacted to the news that the war was over in November 1918. Why do you think they reacted like this?

5. How would you expect Source D to differ if it had been written by a British general?

2 LEGACY OF WORLD WAR I

Lenin, the first Communist leader of Russia

Lloyd George (Prime Minister of Britain), Orlando (Prime Minister of Italy), Clemenceau (Prime Minister of France) and President Wilson of the USA at the Paris Peace Conference in 1919

Themes

Perhaps the two most important outcomes of the First World War were the Russian revolution of 1917 and the peace settlement of 1919.

The Russian revolution of 1917 resulted in the creation of the first Communist government in the world. For several decades before 1914 governments throughout Europe had been afraid of the spread of Communism. After 1917 there was a widespread fear that revolutions like that in Russia would happen elsewhere.

In January 1919 the victorious Allies (Britain, France, the USA and Italy) met in Paris to write Peace Treaties. The countries defeated in the war were forced to sign them. Although the Peace Treaties were designed to produce lasting peace in Europe, they failed to do this.

The fear of Communism and the failure of the peace settlement led to the growth of a new political movement – Fascism. Fascism first gained support in Italy.

This chapter looks at Europe after the First World War and asks these questions.

- Why was there a revolution in Russia?

- What impact did the revolution have on Europe after the First World War?

- What were the terms of the Peace Treaties? Why did they fail?

- What is Fascism?

Focus Activities

1. Karl Marx died in 1883 but the idea of Communism has played an important part in the history of the 20th century.

   a) Explain what Marx believed would have to happen before there could be Communism.

   b) Who would gain from Communism and who would lose? How would they gain or lose?

   c) Why do you think many governments feared Communism?

2. Suppose you either (a) support or (b) oppose the ideas of Karl Marx. Write and illustrate a leaflet explaining what you think of Communism.

The world according to Karl Marx

Communism was the idea of Karl Marx (1818-83). He believed that one day everybody in the whole world would be a Communist. This page shows what he meant by this.

1. Industrial society is divided into two main groups. At the top is the 'ruling class'– people who own businesses and the land. At the bottom is the 'working class' – people who work in factories and on the land. In time, the workers become fed up because they remain poor no matter how hard they work. The ruling class has money and power but refuses to share them with the workers.

2.

Eventually, the workers become so fed up that they start a revolution. Its aim is to make things more equal. Money and power are to be shared between everybody. Different classes will no longer exist. There are two phases in the revolution. First the workers take control of government and work out how best to share out money and power.

3.

Second, as things become more equal, there is no need for government. People share things without being told to do so. This is Communism.

4.

A successful revolution in one country leads to revolutions in other countries. The result is a world revolution followed by world Communism.

The Russian revolution

Until 1917 Russia was ruled by the Tsar, a monarch with absolute power. Supporters of the Tsar claimed that he was a ruler chosen by God and was the 'little father of the people'.

In the early 20th century opponents of Tsarist rule began to question his right to rule. After Russia was defeated in a war against Japan in 1905, there were demonstrations and it seemed that the Tsar would be overthrown. The Tsar avoided this by promising to set up a Parliament.

Although a Parliament was set up, the Tsar refused to listen to its demands. This soon led to discontent. Opponents claimed that the Tsar was out of touch, uncaring and unable to understand the problems of ordinary people. When the First World War broke out in 1914 the Tsar hoped that success in the war would bring him popularity. In fact the war led to revolution and his downfall.

Source B   The Tsar

The last Tsar, Nicholas II

The Tsar is the source of all our misfortunes. He is incapable of steering the ship of state into a quiet harbour. This is what he thinks, 'I do as I please and what I please is good. If ordinary people do not understand it, that is because they are ordinary mortals whereas I was appointed by God.'

Witte, the Tsar's Finance Minister between 1892 and 1903

Source A   The peasants

The majority of Russians were poor peasants. This picture shows how poor they were. These peasants do not have enough food for their animals, so they are feeding them with thatch off their roof. Many peasants wanted to own enough land to feed their family and animals properly. But most land was owned by rich aristocrats who lived off the rents paid by the peasants.

Source C   The workers

Industrialisation began much later in Russia than in Western Europe. Working conditions in new industrial towns were hard. Pay was very low. Although strikes and demonstrations were illegal, they often took place. The result of one strike is shown above. The strikers were shot by the Tsar's soldiers. This made many workers bitter.

Number of strikes 1910-17			
1910	8	1914* (Aug-Dec)	61
1911	24	1915	819
1912	300	1916	1167
1913	1034	1917	1330
1914* (Jan-July)	1560		

* Russia entered the war in August 1914.

Before the First World War the Tsar had been able to rely on the support of the army. The soldiers obeyed the Tsar even if he ordered them to shoot demonstrators. But when the First World War broke out, many new soldiers were recruited. Most were peasants. At first these soldiers remained loyal. But soon things began to go wrong. The German soldiers were better equipped and trained than the Russians. The Russian army was defeated in several battles. In 1915 the Tsar made the decision to take command of the army personally. As a result he was blamed for Russia's defeats. By 1917 many soldiers were no longer prepared to obey him.

Source D   Russia and World War I

Russian soldiers deserting

Size of army		Casualties by 1917	
1913	1.4 million	Dead	0.8 million
1914	6.5 million	Wounded	4.6 million
1917	15.4 million	Captured	3.3 million

In December 1914 Russia had 4.7 million rifles to issue to 6.5 million soldiers on the front line.

The close relations between the factory workers of Petrograd (capital of Russia) and the army is disturbing, not to say revolutionary. There is a high cost of living and a shortage of foodstuffs in the towns. The soldiers' wives are the first to suffer. This is made known to the army by soldiers returning from leave.

Police Department Report, October 1916

Source E   The February revolution

Women queuing for bread in Petrograd, 1917

On February 23rd 1917, International Women's Day, women in Petrograd demonstrated about food shortages. Workers went on strike and joined them. Over the next week the demonstration turned into a revolution. When the Tsar ordered soldiers to shoot the demonstrators, some did but most refused to open fire. Many soldiers joined the demonstrators in demanding an end to Tsarist rule. By the beginning of March the Tsar had lost control. He resigned.

Activities

1. a) Using the sources on these pages make a list of reasons why there was a revolution in Russia in February 1917.

    b) Would you describe each reason as 'short term' or 'long term'? Explain your answers.

2. What evidence is there in Sources A and C to support Witte's view of the Tsar in Source B?

3. Using Sources C, D and E describe the impact of World War I on Russia.

4. Suppose you were a Russian soldier who disobeyed orders in February 1917 (Source E). Write a letter to the Tsar explaining what you did and why.

Communist victory, October 1917

The February revolution was not planned. It happened because enough people (especially soldiers) were so fed up with the Tsar that they were able to force him to resign. Without the support of his soldiers the Tsar had no power. Although the revolution was not planned, many groups had been working for revolution for many years. One of these groups was the Communist Party (set up in 1898). Although the Tsar had banned the Party, Communists met in secret and continued to spread the ideas of Karl Marx (see Focus). When war broke out in 1914 the Communist Party was the only group to argue that Russia should not join in. By 1917, after Russia's defeats, this policy was very popular.

After the February revolution a group of unelected politicians announced that they had formed a 'provisional government' which would take charge until a new political system could be agreed upon. The Communists were the only group to oppose the provisional government. Between May and October support for the Communists grew rapidly. By October they were able to overthrow the provisional government and set up a new Communist government. This is known as the 'October revolution'.

Activities

1. Look at the sources on this page.
   a) Why did the Communists gain support after February 1917?
   b) Why was there a second revolution in October 1917?
   c) How did the second revolution differ from the first?
2. Use the Focus and sources on this page to explain the aims of the Communists after February 1917.

Source A   Lenin

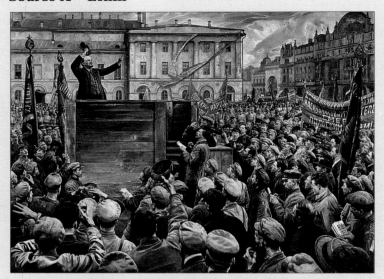

In May 1917 the leader of the Communists, Lenin, returned from exile. This picture shows him arriving in Petrograd. On his arrival he made a speech calling for a second revolution and promising 'peace, bread and land'.

Source B   The provisional government

Promises after February revolution
1. To end the war.
2. To solve food shortages.
3. To hold elections.
4. To give land to the peasants.

Actions by October
1. The war continued. No peace was made.
2. Food shortages continued.
3. No elections were held.
4. No land was given to the peasants.

Source C   The October revolution

On October 24th armed Communists marched to the headquarters of the provisional government, arrested members of the government and set up a new government. During the next few weeks the following actions were taken.

1. The war with Germany was ended and a peace treaty made.
2. Soldiers were sent to find food and bring it to the towns.
3. Peasants were given ownership of land.
4. The death penalty was abolished.
5. Women were given equal rights to men.
6. The workers were given control of factories.
7. All political parties (except the Communist Party) were banned.
8. Newspapers opposed to the Communists were banned.

The 'Red' threat

Although the Communists had the support of many people when they seized power in October 1917, they also had many opponents. Some opponents supported the Tsar or the provisional government. Some supported other political parties. The Communists became known as the 'Reds' (because of the colour of their flag). Their opponents became known as the 'Whites' (because most came from an area known as 'White Russia').

In March 1918 the Communists signed a peace treaty with Germany. This meant the end of Russia's involvement in the First World War. But it did not mean an end to fighting in Russia. The Whites took up arms against the Reds in 1918 and a civil war began. It was won by the Communists in 1922.

Britain, France, the USA and Japan all sent soldiers to help the Whites. They did this because they were angry that the Communists had made peace with Germany and because they were scared that the Russian revolution would spread to other countries.

Source A   Attempted revolutions 1918-23

Distribution of guns to German Communists during the attempted revolution in November 1918

After October 1917 Russian Communist leaders sent letters to Communists in other countries urging them to overthrow their governments. Between 1918 and 1923 there were attempted revolutions in Germany, Hungary, Italy and Bulgaria. All failed because soldiers refused to join the revolution.

Source B

Communists everywhere! Support every revolutionary movement. Let the ruling classes tremble at a Communist revolution. The workers have nothing to lose but their chains. WORKERS OF ALL COUNTRIES UNITE!

K. Marx and F. Engels, 'The Communist Manifesto', 1872

The world Communist revolution has begun.

Pravda (the Russian Communist newspaper), January 1919

Source C   Comintern

In 1919 Comintern (Communist International) was set up by the Russian Communists to encourage world revolution. Comintern gave money to Communist Parties abroad and provided arms and advisers. This poster was produced by Comintern in 1920.

Activities

1. Look at the Focus and the sources on this page.
   a) Explain why foreign governments were scared that the Russian revolution would spread to other countries.
   b) Explain why foreign governments sent soldiers to Russia to fight against the Communists in the civil war.
   c) Suppose that you were one of the Russian Communist leaders in 1917. Write one of the letters mentioned in Source B. Explain in your letter what you hope to achieve.

The Paris Peace Conference

The Russian revolution took place before the end of the First World War. The remaining Allies were not able to force Germany to surrender until November 1918.

Between January and June 1919 politicians from the winning side met at the Paris Peace Conference to decide what should happen to the defeated countries. Britain, France and the USA made most of the important decisions. The defeated countries were not invited to attend the Peace Conference. Nor was the new Russian government. Although Russia had fought on the winning side, it had made peace with Germany before the war was over. The Allies regarded this as a betrayal of their alliance.

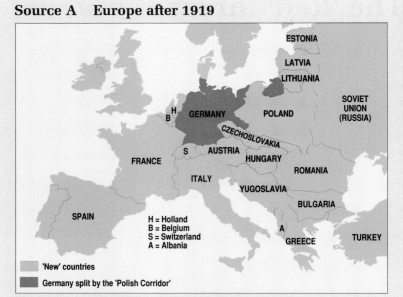

Source A   Europe after 1919

'New' countries

Germany split by the 'Polish Corridor'

At the end of the war the map of Europe was redrawn. Land which had, in 1914, belonged to Germany, Austria-Hungary, Russia and Turkey was divided up. New countries and new frontiers of existing countries were created.

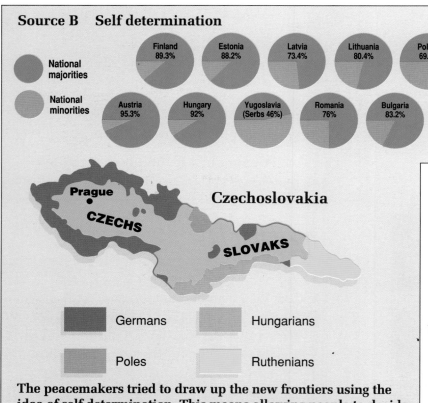

Source B   Self determination

National majorities

National minorities

Finland 89.3% · Estonia 88.2% · Latvia 73.4% · Lithuania 80.4% · Poland 69.1% · Czechoslovakia (Czechs 46%)

Austria 95.3% · Hungary 92% · Yugoslavia (Serbs 46%) · Romania 76% · Bulgaria 83.2% · Albania 92% · Greece 96%

(Czechs are the largest national group in Czechoslovakia. Serbs are the largest national group in Yugoslavia)

Prague · CZECHS · Czechoslovakia · SLOVAKS

Germans · Hungarians

Poles · Ruthenians

The peacemakers tried to draw up the new frontiers using the idea of self determination. This means allowing people to decide (determine) their own future. The aim was to divide Europe into blocks of people who came from a single 'nationality' (a nationality was defined as a group of people who speak the same language and share the same historical and ethnic roots). The information above shows that self determination was more difficult than the peacemakers supposed.

Activities

1. Compare the map on page 4 with the sources on this page. How did Europe change? Who gained and who lost out?

2. Using Source B list the advantages and disadvantages of self determination.

3. Suppose you were a German living in Czechoslovakia in the 1920s. Using Source B write a letter to your government explaining what you thought about the creation of this new country in 1919.

The League of Nations

The peacemakers were not just concerned about Europe. They wanted lasting peace throughout the whole world. To make this more likely they set up the League of Nations – the first ever truly international organisation. The idea was that all countries in the world would join the League. If there was a dispute between two countries, the League would decide which country was in the right. Also if a country committed a 'crime' against another country (for example, by invading it), all the other members of the League would join together and take action against the country which had broken international law. The League was the idea of President Wilson of the USA. But the USA never joined it.

Source B   Membership of the League of Nations

Source C   A British cartoon drawn in 1919

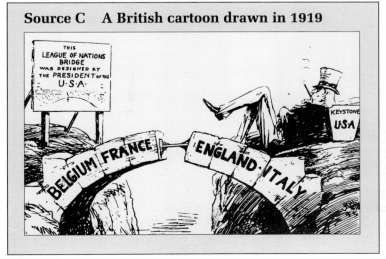

Activities

1. Look at the sources on this page.
   a) Describe the aims of the League.
   b) Explain why the League was weaker than it might have been.

2. Explain how Source B illustrates some of the problems listed in Source A.

3. The cartoon in source C is called 'The gap in the bridge'. What point do you think the cartoonist is making? Use Sources A and B in your answer.

The Treaty of Versailles

In 1871 a war between France and Germany had resulted in victory for the Germans and a German Emperor was crowned in the French palace of Versailles. The memory of this French defeat cast a shadow over the Paris Peace Conference. It is no coincidence that the defeated Germans were required to come to Versailles in June 1919 to sign a peace treaty (the Treaty of Versailles).

The French Prime Minister, Clemenceau, was determined to prevent the Germans ever invading France again. Although the Americans and British were less hard on the Germans, they agreed to measures that weakened Germany.

By June 1919 a new parliamentary democracy had been set up in Germany (the Weimar Republic). This new government had not been responsible for Germany's behaviour during the war but it had to sign the Treaty of Versailles. Many Germans felt that the measures in the Treaty were unfair and too harsh.

Source A   Versailles, 1871

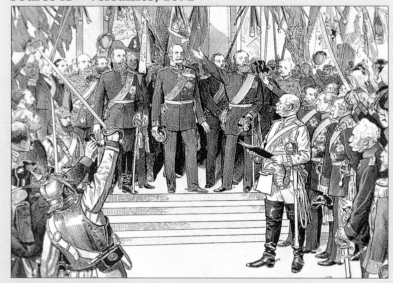

This painting shows the ceremony at Versailles in 1871 when William was made Emperor of Germany.

Source B   Britain's aims at Versailles

Our first task must be to conclude a just and lasting peace.

We must demand the whole cost of the war from Germany.

Comments made by Prime Minister David Lloyd George during the British election campaign, 1918

Source C   Versailles, 1919

This painting shows the signing of the Treaty of Versailles in 1919. The man signing is a representative of the new German government. Opposite him are the representatives of the victorious Allies.

Source D   The Treaty of Versailles

Germany agrees:

1. to accept the new frontiers and to keep the peace
2. to accept decisions made by the League of Nations
3. to limit the size of its army and navy
4. to give up its Empire
5. to accept the blame for starting the war and to pay compensation* to countries that suffered damage in the war.

Extracts from the Treaty of Versailles, 1919

* This compensation was later set at £6,600 million and was to be paid in cash and materials.

Source E Reactions to the Treaty of Versailles

VENGEANCE, GERMAN NATION!
Today in the palace of Versailles, the disgraceful treaty is being signed. Do not forget it. The German people will reconquer the place among the nations to which they are entitled. Then will come vengeance for the shame of 1919.

Deutsche Zeitung (a German newspaper), 28 June 1919

This is not peace. It is a ceasefire that will last for no more than twenty years.

Marshal Foch, a senior French soldier, 1919

The Treaty is not just stern it is actually punitive (a severe punishment). If I were the Germans I shouldn't sign it for a minute.

Entry in the diary of Harold Nicholson (a British civil servant at the Paris Peace Conference), 1919

Source F Cartoon drawn in 1919

Ghosts at Versailles

Source G Economic crisis in Germany 1922-4

In 1922 prices began to rise so quickly that the German Mark became virtually worthless. In this picture, taken in 1923, children are playing with bundles of banknotes which are worth practically nothing.

A 100,000,000 Mark note dated 25 September 1923

Value of German currency in relation to the dollar	
1914:	4.2
1919:	14.0
1921:	76.7
August 1923:	4,620,455.0
November 1923:	4,200,000,000,000.0

Activities

1. Use Sources A and C to explain the point that is being made in the cartoon in Source F.

2. Look at Sources B and D. Would you say that the Treaty fulfilled Britain's aims? Explain your answer.

3. Using Source D explain the reactions in Source E.

4. 'The Treaty of Versailles and the economic crisis caused resentment and hardship in Germany.' Explain using Sources D, E and G.

Italy and the rise of Fascism

When the First World War broke out in 1914, Italy was neutral. But in 1915 Britain and France promised Italy new territory if it joined them in the war. The Italian government was tempted. It signed the Treaty of London and Italy joined the war on the side of the Allies. Although Italy fought on the winning side, over half a million Italian soldiers were killed in the war.

After the war a mood of triumph in Italy quickly turned into discontent. The promises made in 1915 were not kept. There was an economic crisis. The government appeared weak. As a result many people wondered whether it had been worth fighting in the war. They blamed the government for the problems that had arisen and began to look for new leaders. Some joined the Italian Communist Party. Others supported a new party – the Fascist Party.

Source A   Italy and the Paris Peace Conference

Key:
- Territory gained by Italy in 1919
- Territory claimed by Italy but not gained in 1919

In 1915 in the Treaty of London Britain and France promised Italy South Tyrol, Dalmatia, Albania and overseas territory. But at the Paris Peace Conference the American President, Wilson, argued that self determination should be used to draw new frontiers. The result was that, although Italy was given South Tyrol and other small areas, the other promises in the Treaty were ignored.

Source B

Victory in the war was achieved with untold hardship. Then Italy was betrayed at the Paris Peace Conference. This shattered the hopes of the Italians. We lost the whole of Dalmatia. Dalmatia is our land by tradition and history, by manners and custom, by language and by the desire of the Dalmatians. I could feel the discontent oozing down through our masses.

Benito Mussolini, autobiography, 1928

Source D   The Fascist symbol

The word 'Fascist' comes from the Latin 'fasces'. The fasces were bundles of rods and axes carried in front of the ancient Roman Consuls. These bundles were a symbol of the Consul's power of life and death over Roman citizens. By choosing the name 'Fascist' for his new political movement Mussolini made it clear that the Fascists had links with Italy's glorious past and that they stood for law and order.

Source C   Birth of Fascism

The Fascist movement was set up by Benito Mussolini in March 1919. He argued that the government had failed and a new approach was needed. He promised to destroy Communism in Italy and make Italy great again.

This poster shows the Fascist leaders in the 1920s. Mussolini is at the top. Many of the first people to join the Fascist party were ex-soldiers who had found it difficult to find jobs after the war and felt that the government had let them down. The Fascists wore black uniforms and became known as 'blackshirts'.

Source E   A Fascist postcard

This postcard reads, '1919 Communism; 1923 Fascism'.

Between 1919 and 1922 Italian Communists organised strikes and demonstrations in the hope that this would lead to a Communist revolution like that in Russia. In 1919 1.5 million workers went on strike. The next year the number rose to over 2 million. When the government refused to take action, the Fascists took matters into their own hands. Groups of Fascists attacked workers and forced them to go back to work. Factory owners and other people afraid of a Communist revolution welcomed this and support for the Fascists grew.

Source F   Number of Fascists

Dec 1919	870	Dec 1921	218,000
Dec 1920	20,000	May 1922	332,000
Mar 1921	80,000		

Source G

I felt we had to destroy everything to build it up again from the bottom. Many at that time joined the Communists because they wanted revolution. Without Mussolini, most of the soldiers returning from the war would have become Communists.

Entry in the diary of Italo Balbo (a Fascist leader), 1922

Source H

The Fascists would strike without warning at night. They would beat their opponents. Communist peasants would be left chained naked to trees whilst their attackers went home singing.

Sandro Carosi was a Fascist in the Pisa area. One day he and a couple of others went into an inn where Communist peasants met. There was an uneasy silence. In the spirit of 'fun' Carosi lined a peasant against a wall, placed an apple on his head and fired at it. He killed the peasant. No one dared do anything.

A. Lyttleton, 'The Seizure of Power: Fascism in Italy 1919-1929', 1973

Source I

Our programme is simple: we wish to govern Italy. We will govern it as it has never been governed since Roman times – firmly, fairly, justly, honestly and, above all, efficiently.

Benito Mussolini, autobiography, 1928

Activities

1. Using the sources on these pages explain:
   a) why Mussolini set up the Fascist Party
   b) who joined the Party
   c) why they joined.
2. Using Sources A, B and E explain why there was discontent in Italy after the war.
3. Look at Sources B and C. Why do you think that the Fascist Party appealed to ex-soldiers?
4. Look at Sources D, E, G and I. What were the aims of the Fascist Party?
5. What does Source H tell us about the tactics used by the Fascist Party?

Italian Fascism

The Italian Fascist Party was not elected to power nor did it gain power by force. It bluffed its way into power. In October 1922 Mussolini planned a march on Rome. Fascists from all over Italy were to gather outside the gates and march into the city. When news of this reached Rome, the government panicked (fearing civil war) and resigned. King Victor Emmanuel III (Italy's head of state) then invited Mussolini to become Prime Minister. Mussolini accepted. The next day about 30,000 Fascists arrived in Rome and marched triumphantly through the streets. Later Mussolini invented the story that he rode into Rome on horseback at the head of 300,000 armed Fascists. They had, he said, come to Rome to rescue the government from civil war.

   Once he had become Prime Minister, Mussolini took measures to make sure that the Fascists would not lose power. He described his rule as a 'Fascist revolution' and called himself 'il Duce' (the leader).

Source B   Fascist propaganda

Most Fascist propaganda focused on Mussolini. He was shown as a strong and successful leader who cared about his people. Here Mussolini, imitating Romulus the founder of Rome, is seen helping to drain the Pontine marshes so a new city could be built – the ancient Romans had tried and failed to drain the Pontine marshes.

Source D

I believe in the genius of Mussolini, in our holy Father Fascism and in the rebirth of the Roman Empire.

Oath taken by members of the Fascist Youth Movement

Source A   Dictatorship

Mussolini in a typical pose

In April 1923 Mussolini persuaded the Italian Parliament to pass a new electoral law. The party with most votes would now automatically gain two thirds of the seats in Parliament. (Before 1923 the electoral system prevented any one party gaining a majority of seats.) Elections were held in April 1924. The Fascists and their allies won 66% of the votes. They now had control of Parliament. In May 1924 an opposition MP, Matteoti, claimed that the election had been corrupt. In June he was murdered by Fascists. Mussolini did not deny responsibility for this and in January 1925 took measures to silence opposition. Opposition newspapers were closed and all political parties (except the Fascist Party) were banned. Italy had become a one party state. Mussolini was free to rule as a dictator.

Source C

We are becoming a military nation. We believe in the virtues of obedience, sacrifice and dedication to our country. That means that the whole life of the nation must be directed towards our military requirements.

Speech made by Mussolini in 1934

Source E   The impact of Fascism

Mussolini was Europe's first postwar dictator. The success of Italian Fascism in the 1920s had an effect on other countries. Other would-be dictators copied Mussolini's style and tactics. This postcard shows Mussolini as the Roman wolf which nursed Romulus and Remus (the mythical founders of Rome). The wolf is suckling Hitler (Chancellor of Germany from 1933), Attaturk (President of Turkey from 1923), Metaxas (Greek Prime Minister from 1936), Franco (ruler of Spain from 1939) and Oswald Moseley (leader of the British Union of Fascists). All five aimed to create a one party state like that in Italy.

Checklist

- Before the end of the First World War there was a revolution in Russia. The Tsar resigned in March 1917. The Communists gained power in October.

- At the Paris Peace Conference in 1919 the Allies tried to make sure there would be lasting peace in Europe. But the Treaty of Versailles was very hard on Germany and the idea of self determination caused problems.

- Discontent with the peace settlement, an economic crisis and fear of Communism led to the growth of Fascism in Italy. Mussolini became Europe's first postwar dictator.

Activities

1. What do Sources A, C and D tell us about Mussolini's aims after he had gained power?

2. Look at Source B.

   a) Why do you think that Mussolini wanted to drain the Pontine marshes?

   b) Would you describe the photo in Source B as a successful piece of propaganda? Explain your answer.

   c) What does this source tell us about the type of government Mussolini headed?

3. Using Sources C, D and E explain why lasting peace in Europe was less likely once the Fascists had gained power in Italy.

4. Look at Source E.

   a) What point is being made by the cartoonist?

   b) What does the cartoon tell us about the impact of Italian Fascism?

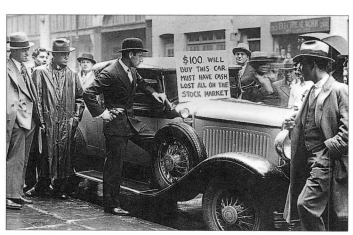

USA – car for sale after the Stock Market collapse

Britain – unemployed men scratching for pieces of coal on a slag heap

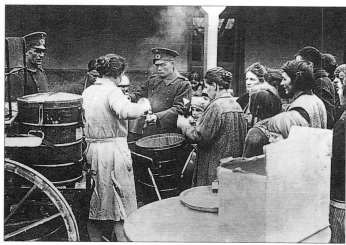

Germany – soldiers serving soup to the unemployed

Themes

In October 1929 the price of shares on the American Stock Market collapsed. The USA was plunged into an economic depression which spread rapidly to the rest of the world. Later this became known as the 'Great Depression'.

Massive unemployment and widespread poverty made people desperate throughout the 1930s. Some saw Communism as the answer to their problems. Others turned to dictators. In 1933 Adolf Hitler's Nazi party gained power in Germany. By 1939 there were few democracies left in Europe.

Hopes of peace based on cooperation through the League of Nations faded. Rearmament created jobs but it also threatened peace. Dictators became popular by appearing tough and aggressive but this made war more likely.

This chapter looks at Europe in the 1930s and asks:

- How did the rise to power of Hitler in Germany and Stalin in Russia affect the stability of Europe?

- Why did attempts to keep the peace fail?

Focus Activities

1. Look at the pictures on this page and the Focus.
   a) Explain what it was like to be unemployed during the Great Depression.
   b) What evidence is there that this was a *world* depression?

2. What does the election poster in the Focus tell us about British people's concerns in the 1931 election?

20

Unemployment and the Great Depression

The Great Depression caused massive unemployment across the world. It brought great misery to many people and made them discontented with their governments. In Britain and the USA governments changed but parliamentary democracy survived. In Germany parliamentary democracy did not survive – discontent with the government led to support for opponents of parliamentary democracy, the Nazis and Communists.

A. British views

1. This afternoon I went to see the unemployed miners scrambling for coal. It was a most astonishing sight. The train came round the bend at 20 mph and between 50 and 70 men rushed for it, hoisting themselves onto the trucks. As soon as the train stopped at the dirt heap, the men started shovelling and sorting through the dirt. They put small lumps of coal into their sacks. Later, they sold the coal for 1s 6d (7½p) per bag.

   Extract from George Orwell's diary, 1936

2. The unemployed on the dole often looked for cheap luxuries. Gambling on the football pools was the cheapest. I was in Yorkshire when Hitler reoccupied the Rhineland (see page 31). The threat of war hardly raised a flicker of interest but the decision not to publish the football fixtures in advance caused a storm.

   George Orwell, 'The Road to Wigan Pier', 1937

B. German views

1. I met a poor family where the man had been unemployed for a year. His allowance had gone down to 30s (£1.50) per week – for himself, his wife and nine children. They were living in two small rooms. Three cabbages for their daily meal were simmering in the pot.

   F.Y. Brown, 'The Spectator', 1932

2. With over half of all Germans between the ages of 16 and 30 unemployed, young Germans were easy victims for a rabble rouser.

   E. Mowrer, 'Germany Puts the Clock Back', 1933

C. American views

1. I was out of work for six months. I was losing my energy. One of the worst things was to occupy your time sensibly. I didn't have a radio. I tried to read but couldn't concentrate. So I just vegetated.

   S. Terkel, 'Hard Times', 1970 – an interview with a 73 year old teacher

2. There was a feeling we were on the verge of a revolution. Many people worked with the Communist Party but the New Deal stopped this. (The New Deal was a series of government measures designed to reduce unemployment and to end the Depression. The New Deal was introduced by President Roosevelt, the first President to be elected from the Democratic Party since World War I. See page 54.)

   S. Terkel, 'Hard Times', 1970

Smokeless Chimneys and – ANXIOUS MOTHERS!

THE REMEDY

VOTE FOR THE NATIONAL GOVERNMENT

A poster produced for the British election held during the Great Depression, in October 1931. In Britain a Labour government was elected in 1929. By 1931 the Depression was so bad that the Labour leaders invited Conservatives to join the government in a coalition. This coalition – the 'National Government' – won the election of 1931 and governed Britain until 1935.

The Nazis

Germany's new parliamentary democracy – the Weimar Republic – lasted for just 14 years (1919-1933). Not only did it suffer from economic problems (see page 15), it also had many opponents. Among these was Adolf Hitler who in 1919 left the German army, bitter about its defeat. In 1920 he became Member 55 of a small political group called the National Socialist German Workers Party (The Nazis). By the end of 1920 the Nazi Party had just 2,000 members. But by 1933 Hitler was able to lead the Nazis to power.

Source B   The Nazis' aims

It must be a greater honour to be a street cleaner and a citizen of this country than a king in a foreign state.

The question of the future of the German nation is the question of destroying Communism.

Adolf Hitler, 'Mein Kampf', 1924

First, the people must be taught fanatical Nationalism (patriotism). Second, we must educate them to fight against the insanity of democracy. We must teach them the nonsense of Parliament and to recognise authority and leadership. Third, we must destroy people's pitiable belief in possibilities such as world peace, the League of Nations and international cooperation.

Adolf Hitler, speech to Nazi Party leaders, 23 September 1928

Source A   Failure and reassessment

HITLER's
MEIN KAMPF

THE BLUE-PRINT OF GERMAN IMPERIALISM

THE MOST WIDELY DISCUSSED BOOK OF THE MODERN WORLD

ROYALTIES ON ALL SALES WILL GO TO ✚ THE BRITISH RED CROSS SOCIETY

illustrated by 200 FULL PAGE PLATES

The original Edition entirely UNEXPURGATED 6D NET

English translation of 'Mein Kampf'

In November 1923 the Nazis in Munich tried and failed to take power by force. They failed because the army and local leaders refused to join them. Hitler was arrested and sentenced to 5 years in prison (he was released after 9 months). Whilst in prison Hitler wrote 'Mein Kampf' ('My Struggle'), a book which set out the Nazis' aims. After Hitler's release, the Nazis no longer aimed to win power by force. They began to work for mass support and to win seats in the Reichstag (German Parliament).

Source C   Effects of the Great Depression

On top of the defeat in World War I and the inflation of 1923-24 came the Depression. Like men and women in a town stricken by an earthquake, millions of Germans saw the apparently solid framework of their existence cracking and crumbling. In such circumstances people no longer listen to reason. They have fantastic fears, extravagant hatreds and extravagant hopes. In such circumstances the speeches of Hitler began to attract a mass following as they had never done before.

A. Bullock, 'Hitler - A Study in Tyranny', 1962

Source D   Unemployment in Germany

Unemployment (in millions)

Nov 1929	1.7
Nov 1930	3.3
Nov 1931	4.7
Nov 1932	5.1

Source E   Winning support

Hitler saluting from a car

Like Mussolini's Fascists, the Nazis adopted a military style. Rallies were held all over Germany. They showed how well the party was organised and how strong it was. Hitler was a skillful speaker. His appearance at rallies roused his supporters and developed his image as a leader, as this passage shows.

Listening to Hitler in 1922, an admirer said, 'I was held under a hypnotic spell. The will of the man seemed to flow into me. It was like a religious conversion.'

Kurt Ludecke quoted in I. Kershaw, 'Hitler', 1991

Source H   Hitler as Chancellor

People not taking part in the election campaign should at least make financial sacrifices. The sacrifices asked for are easier to bear if it is realised that the election will be the last for at least the next 10 years, probably even for the next 100 years.

Speech made by Goering (Hitler's deputy) to rich industrialists, 20 February 1933

Source F   Support for the Nazis in elections

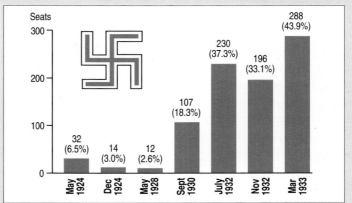

The figures above each bar show the number of Nazi MPs and their percentage of the total vote (in brackets). From July 1932 the Nazis were the single largest party.

Source G   Hitler becomes Chancellor

Hitler at a rally in Dortmund, 1933

In the Weimar Republic no party ever gained more than 50% of MPs, so several parties had to combine to form a government. Before 1933 other parties had been able to join together to keep the Nazis out of government. But after the November 1932 election Hitler was able to make a deal. In January 1933 he was appointed Chancellor (Prime Minister). Like Mussolini in Italy, once Hitler had power, he was determined to keep it.

Activities

1. Look at Source A. Why was 1923 a turning point in Hitler's career?
2. What does Source B tell us about the aims of the Nazis?
3. Look at Sources C, D and E. Why did the Nazis gain support?
4. Look at Sources F and G. The Nazis claimed that they were swept to power on a wave of popular support. Is this true? Explain your answer.
5. What does Source H tell us about what the Nazis intended to do after the election in March 1933? Judging from Sources B and F, why do you think they intended this?

Hitler in power

Hitler's appointment as Chancellor meant the end of the Weimar Republic and the beginning of the 'Third Reich'. Hitler moved quickly and ruthlessly to remove all opposition to the Nazis, including any possible rivals to himself within the Nazi Party. He then built up his power, attempting to win the support of as many people as possible.

Source B   The Enabling Law

The 'respectable face' of Hitler. He sits next to the German President, Hindenberg.

Although the Nazis won just 288 out of 647 seats in the March 1933 election, the Enabling Law was passed in April by 444 votes to 44. This law transferred the power to make laws from the Reichstag to the Cabinet. In practice this meant that Hitler alone was now responsible for making new laws.

Source C   The destruction of opposition

After the Enabling Law had been passed in 1933, political opponents (mainly Communists) were rounded up and sent to concentration camps which were first set up that year. Newspapers were closed, all political parties except the Nazi Party were banned and trade unions were replaced by organisations run by the Nazis.

Source A   The Reichstag Fire

As soon as he was appointed Chancellor in January 1933, Hitler called for elections to be held in March. In February the Reichstag (Parliament building) was burned down. A Dutch Communist was tried and executed for starting the blaze.

The Reichstag burning, February 1933

I can only repeat that I set fire to the Reichstag all by myself.

Van Der Lubbe, the Dutchman arrested for starting the fire, at his trial in 1933

At lunch on the birthday of the Fuhrer (Hitler) in 1942, the conversation turned to the Reichstag. Goering (Hitler's deputy) shouted, 'The only one who really knows about the Reichstag is me because I set it on fire'.

G. Halder, a German general, 1946

In the time available, it would have been impossible for one man to set the building alight in so many places, especially a man mentally and physically handicapped like Van Der Lubbe.

R. Manvell and H. Fraenkel, 'The Hundred Days to Hitler', 1974

The burning of the Reichstag was to have been the signal for bloody uprising by the Communists.

German Government statement, February 1933

The mysterious fire, a few days before the election, was blamed on the Communists and used as an excuse for banning free speech.

J. M. Roberts, 'Europe 1880-1945', 1970

Source D 'The Night of the Long Knives'

THEY SALUTE WITH BOTH HANDS NOW

Hitler Göbbels Göring

With all opposition parties abolished, Hitler turned against the Stormtroopers (SA), the Nazis' private army. They were a possible threat to Hitler's power. On the night of 30 June 1934 between 150 and 200 members of the SA were shot. The British cartoon above shows the SA on the left and the regular army top right. Hitler, Goering (his deputy) and Goebbels (the Minister for Propaganda) are pictured in the foreground.

Source F Solving unemployment

Opening ceremony for an autobahn

Germany had a weak economy and high unemployment when Hitler came to power. One of his solutions was to build autobahns (motorways). This provided employment and also helped the Nazis' military preparations (troops and equipment could be easily moved).

Source E Propaganda

The Nazis saw the importance of persuading people, especially the young, that Hitler would make Germany a great power once again.

Ein Volk, ein Reich, ein Führer!

This poster reads, 'One People, one State, one Leader!' Hitler was given the title 'Fuhrer' (leader).

Cut out figures of Stormtroopers for children

Activities

1. Use Source A to explain who you think started the Reichstag fire, and why.

2. What do Sources B, C and D tell you about Hitler's aims after he became Chancellor?

3. Explain what the cartoon in Source D was trying to show.

4. What was the purpose of the pictures in Source E? Do you think they would have been effective? Give reasons for your answers.

5. Would the Nazi policy in Source F have been popular with most Germans? Explain your answer.

Stalin's rise to power

Joseph Stalin was one of the leading Communists at the time of the Russian revolution. Together with Leon Trotsky and other members of the Politburo (The Communist Party's Cabinet), he helped Lenin to plan and organise the seizure of power by the Communists in October 1917. Lenin remained in charge of the government in Russia (or the Soviet Union as it became known after the revolution) until he suffered a stroke in 1922. Following his stroke there was a struggle for power. Stalin used his position as General Secretary of the Communist Party to defeat his main rival, Trotsky. Trotsky was forced into exile. Stalin then set out to make the Soviet Union a strong industrial nation. During the 1920s and 1930s the Soviet Union was the only Communist country in the world. Stalin's policies were designed to show the rest of the world that Communism could be successful in one country even without a world revolution.

Source A   Lenin's will

In 1923 Lenin, ill and near to death, knew that Stalin might try to become leader in his place. This worried Lenin, as his will shows. After Lenin's death Stalin made sure that the will was never made public.

Comrade Stalin, as General Secretary, has great power and I am not sure that he always knows how to use it with sufficient caution. He is too rude. Therefore, I suggest that comrades remove Stalin from this position and appoint a man more loyal, more patient, more polite and more attentive to comrades.

Lenin's will, 1923

Source B   The removal of a rival

Leon Trotsky had organised the Red army during the civil war of 1918-1922. This brought him fame and popularity outside the Communist Party but he had many enemies within the Party, including Stalin. After Lenin's death in 1924 Trotsky was gradually stripped of his jobs in government. He was exiled in 1929 and killed with an icepick by Stalin's agents in Mexico in 1940.

Leon Trotsky (1879-1940) pictured with an icepick on a Soviet flag

Joseph Stalin (1879-1953)

An historian's view of Stalin

- He kept his thoughts to himself and was good at listening to others.
- He saw which way the wind was blowing and always voted with the majority.
- He played off one group of leaders against another.
- As General Secretary he was reponsible for choosing people to do important jobs in government. He chose his own supporters.
- His ideas seemed less dangerous than Trotsky's.

I. Deutscher, 'Stalin', 1961

Source C   Building up industry

From 1928 a series of 'Five Year Plans' was launched by the government to build up heavy industry (like iron and steel) and to increase production of coal, oil and electricity. All industry was owned by the government.

We are fifty or a hundred years behind the advanced countries. We must make good this lag in ten years. Either we do it or they crush us.

Extract from a speech made by Stalin in 1931

Source E   Industrial production

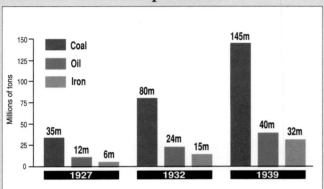

As a result of the Five Year Plans, by 1939 industrial output in the Soviet Union had overtaken that of Britain and was behind only the USA and Germany.

Source G   Verdicts on Stalin's 'Great Change'

The overwhelming majority of peasants opposed collectivisation. Villages were surrounded by machine guns and forced to collectivise. Masses of peasants were deported to Siberia. Others slaughtered cattle, smashed tools and burned crops rather than bring them to the collective farms. Famine stalked the land.

J. Nettl, 'The Soviet Achievement', 1967

J. Scott, an American engineer in Magnitogorsk in the 1930s, wrote, 'I worked in iron and steel. Tens of thousands of people endured intense hardship to build blast furnaces. Many did it willingly with great enthusiasm. Their enthusiasm infected me.'

J. Nettl, 'The Soviet Achievement', 1967

Source D   Collectivisation of agriculture

To feed the industrial workers, Stalin decided to reorganise agriculture. Peasants were forced to work on large 'collective' farms. These farms were owned by the government and each year part of the produce had to be handed over to the government. Peasants were no longer allowed to own land.

A posed photograph of peasants on a collective farm in the Ukraine, 1929

Source F   Agricultural production

Agricultural produce	1928 (before collectivisation)	1932 (after collectivisation)
Cattle (millions)	70.5	40.7
Pigs (millions)	26.0	11.6
Horses (millions)	33.5	19.6
Grain (millions of tons)	73.6	69.6

Activities

1. Look at Sources A and B.

   a) Compare the views of Stalin in these sources.

   b) Explain how Stalin defeated his rivals for power.

2. a) Look at Sources C, D, E, F and G. What effect did Stalin's policies for industry and agriculture have on (i) production and (ii) the lives of ordinary people?

   b) What do these sources tell us about the Soviet Union during the Great Depression?

3. Why do you think the photograph in Source D was taken?

The Spanish Civil War 1936-1939

In 1931 the King of Spain, Alfonso, went into exile and Spain became a republic. For the next five years there was great rivalry between Republicans (supporters of the Republic) and Nationalists (opponents of the Republic).

Republican groups included the Communists and Anarchists (Anarchists believe there should be no government – people should make decisions themselves). Support for Republican groups came mainly from industrial and agricultural workers. Nationalist groups included Fascists and Monarchists. Support for these groups came from wealthy landowners and industrialists, the army and the Catholic Church.

In 1936 Republican groups came together and formed a 'Popular Front' government. This was the signal for a revolt by the Nationalists led by General Franco. Between 1936 and 1939 there was a bitter civil war which ended in victory for General Franco.

The Spanish Civil War had great importance internationally. Hitler and Mussolini sent aid to General Franco. Stalin sent aid to the Republicans. The war was seen as a battle between Fascism and Communism. The Democracies (Britain, France and the USA) refused to interfere, a policy called 'non-intervention'.

Source A   The course of the war

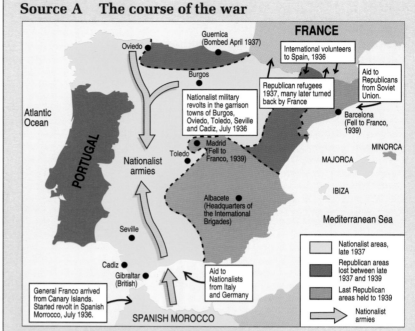

The Nationalists expected a quick victory. Franco led professional soldiers and was helped by his Fascist Allies, Italy and Germany. Although the Republicans received less help from abroad, they managed to resist for three years.

Source B   A Republican poster

Both sides saw the importance of propaganda to encourage support. This poster shows General Franco as the Fascist angel of death armed by Hitler and with his cloak held by a general, a rich industrialist and a Catholic priest.

Source C   The destruction of Guernica

On 26 April 1937 the ancient town of Guernica was bombed by German airplanes. 70% of buildings were destroyed, many by fires caused by incendiary (fire) bombs. Fighter planes flew low over the town machine gunning civilians who were trying to find shelter.

Source D   Help for Franco

Despite agreeing in public to the international policy of non-intervention, Germany and Italy proceeded to help Franco. This picture shows the Condor Legion, a force of 15,000 German troops sent to Spain. Italy sent 60,000 troops. According to Goering (Hitler's Deputy and Head of the Luftwaffe, the German air force), the Germans were sent to stop the spread of Communism and to 'test my young Luftwaffe'.

Source F   British views

My memory is of a poor fellow volunteer in a shabby uniform. The central issue of the war was the attempt of people like this to win a decent life. All that such men ask is enough food to eat, freedom from unemployment, the knowledge that their children will get a fair chance and a roof that does not leak.

George Orwell, 'Looking Back on the Spanish War', 1942

The Spanish Civil War was a chance to make a positive stand on an issue that seemed clear. Either you opposed Fascism and went to fight against it or you allowed its growth.

Jason Gurney, 'Crusade in Spain', 1974

Source E   Help for the Republicans

Opponents of Fascism from all over the world came to Spain to fight on the Republican side as members of the International Brigade. This picture shows a group of British volunteers. The Republicans also received some aid from the Soviet Union – Stalin sent money, weapons and advisers but no troops.

Activities

1. What does Source A tell us about the Spanish Civil War?

2. Look at Source B. Design a poster supporting Franco's Nationalists.

3. Look at Source C. The air raid on Guernica was the first ever to be filmed.

   a) Write an eyewitness account of the raid.

   b) Describe what it was like to see the film of the raid in a British cinema.

4. Look at Sources C, D, E and F.

   a) Explain the importance of foreign intervention in the war.

   b) Why do you think Hitler and Mussolini sent help to Franco?

   c) Why do you think British volunteers went to Spain?

The origins of World War II

In the early 1930s the League of Nations (see page 13) faced two crises. Japan invaded Manchuria (part of China) in 1931 and Italy invaded Abyssinia (modern Ethiopia) in 1935. Both China and Abyssinia appealed to the League for help but it was unable to prevent the conquest of these two areas.

As a result, the League lost face. Japan and Germany left the League in 1933. It was ignored during the Spanish Civil War. Italy left in 1937. By then it was clear that the League was unable to settle disputes. This encouraged dictators like Hitler and Mussolini to become more warlike.

Until 1939 the British and French governments followed a foreign policy known as 'appeasement'. Appeasement means giving in to demands in the hope that a problem can be solved without a fight. By the mid 1930s the British and French governments both agreed that the Treaty of Versailles had been too severe on Germany. They hoped that by 'appeasing' Hitler (giving in to his demands) a major war would be avoided.

Source A   The invasion of Abyssinia

BARBARISM — CIVILIZATION

Mussolini claimed that, 'Italy could above all civilise Africa'. This British cartoon gives a rather different point of view.

Source B

THE AWFUL WARNING.

FRANCE AND ENGLAND (together?).

"WE DON'T WANT YOU TO FIGHT, BUT, BY JINGO, IF YOU DO, WE SHALL PROBABLY ISSUE A JOINT MEMORANDUM SUGGESTING A MILD DISAPPROVAL OF YOU."

Britain and France show 'mild disapproval' of Mussolini's invasion of Abyssinia. Britain and France were leading members of the League but they feared that Mussolini would turn to Hitler for support if they took action against Italy.

Source C

The interests of peace are the same the world over. Any loss of confidence in the League of Nations in any part of the world damages it everywhere.

Lytton Commission Report on Manchuria, 1932

Source D   Sanctions imposed on Italy, 1935

The League condemned Mussolini's aggression and imposed economic sanctions. Members of the League were forbidden to import goods from Italy or to provide loans. The export of raw materials to Italy were stopped. But coal, iron, steel, scrap metal and, most important, oil were left out of the ban.

E.G. Rayner, 'International Affairs', 1983

Source E   German rearmament

The Treaty of Versailles stated that the German army was to be reduced to 100,000 soldiers and Germany must not build military equipment or weapons. But as soon as he gained power Hitler began to build up the German armed forces. In 1933 50,000 new soldiers were called up and Goering announced to the 'Daily Mail' that a new German airforce was being built.

A French cartoon showing Hitler as an angel of peace. 'Pax' means peace.

Source F   The Rhineland

The Treaty of Versailles stated that the Rhineland (the part of Germany bordering France) was to be a demilitarised zone. In March 1936 Hitler sent his army to occupy the Rhineland. Breaking the Treaty was a gamble, but it worked. France and Britain protested but took no action.

Activities

1. What do the cartoons in Sources A and B tell us about Mussolini's invasion of Abyssinia?

2. Look at Sources B, C and D.
   a) Why did the League of Nations fail?
   b) Why were the League's failures important?

3. Explain the British and French policy of appeasement using Sources B, E and F.

4. Look at the picture in Source F. Does it prove that the people of the Rhineland were glad to see German soldiers?

5. Using Sources F and G explain why no action was taken to prevent the German army entering the Rhineland. Could the occupation of the Rhineland have been stopped?

Source G   Views on the occupation of the Rhineland

The French generals were over cautious. They estimated that 90,000 German troops were used to occupy the Rhineland. In fact there were 35,000.
A. Adamthwaite, 'The Making of the Second World War', 1977

If the French had taken action, we would have been easily defeated.
Adolf Hitler

Hitler would certainly have drawn back if we had stood up to him.
Comment made by Charles De Gaulle (French General) after the Second World War

A French attack would have led to a war between France and Germany.
D.C. Watt, an historian, quoted in 'History Today', October 1992

I suppose Jerry (Germany) can do what he likes in his own back yard.
Comment made by a taxi driver to the British Foreign Secretary, 1936

The origins of World War II

By failing to act when Germany broke the terms of the Treaty of Versailles, Britain and France gave Hitler the impression that they would do anything to avoid war. As a result he was prepared to take more risks. By 1938 he was ready to put his plan to create a 'Greater Germany' into action. In March German troops marched into Austria. Austria now became part of Germany. When Britain and France did not act, Hitler then turned to his next target, Czechoslovakia.

Source A   'Greater Germany'

A map from a German atlas published in 1936. Hitler's aim was to unite all German speaking people and those who shared German culture (way of life).

Czechoslovakia was the most successful of the new states set up in 1919. It was a parliamentary democracy with a strong economy. But it had a German minority of 3.5 million. Hitler deliberately stirred up trouble. Nazi supporters amongst the German minority called for union with Germany and the threat of a German invasion grew. Fearing war, the British Prime Minister, Neville Chamberlain, met Hitler three times in 1938. The third meeting at Munich – the Munich Conference – brought peace. But the price of peace was that the Germans were allowed to occupy one part of Czechoslovakia. Again, Hitler had gained exactly what he wanted.

By 1938 Hitler had formed a firm partnership with Mussolini. They had worked together in the Spanish Civil War and formed an alliance called the 'Axis'. Then, in August 1939, Hitler surprised the world by revealing that Germany had made an alliance with his arch enemy, the Soviet Union. Nine days later Germany's invasion of Poland brought the start of World War II.

Source B   Appeasement

If only we could sit down at a table with the Germans and run through all their complaints with a pencil, this would greatly relieve all tension. Herr Hitler's aims are strictly limited. When I think of those four terrible years (1914-18) and of the seven million young men cut off in their prime, I am bound to say again that in war there are no winners but all are losers.

Neville Chamberlain, 1938

Source C   The Czechoslovak crisis

How horrible, fantastic, incredible it is that we should be digging trenches and trying on gas masks here because of a quarrel in a far away country between people of whom we know nothing.

Neville Chamberlain speaking in a radio broadcast two days before the Munich Conference, when war seemed likely

Source D   The results of Munich (1)

Chamberlain returned to Britain from Munich with a document signed by Hitler which seemed to guarantee peace. But in March 1939 Germany occupied the rest of Czechoslovakia. Fearing Poland would be the next to be attacked, the British and French announced they would go to Poland's aid if it was invaded.

> We, the German Fuhrer and Chancellor and the British Prime Minister, have had a further meeting today and are agreed in recognising that the question of Anglo-German relations is of the first importance for the two countries and for Europe.
>
> We are resolved that the method of consultation shall be the method adopted to deal with any other questions that may concern our two countries, and we are determined to continue our efforts to remove possible sources of difference and thus to contribute to assure the peace of Europe.

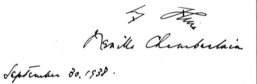

September 30. 1938.

The Anglo-German agreement. Hitler's signature is above Chamberlain's.

Source E   The results of Munich (2)

A British cartoon commenting on the Nazi-Soviet pact of 23 August 1939. The Soviet Union had been ignored at the Munich Conference. Stalin realised that the German advance eastwards (the occupation of Austria and Czechoslovakia) was a threat to the Soviet Union. Seeing no hope of an alliance with Britain and France, Stalin signed a treaty with Hitler. The two countries agreed not to attack each other and to divide Poland. Hitler was now free to invade Poland without fear of being attacked by the Soviet Union. Nine days after the treaty was signed German troops marched into Poland.

Checklist

- The Great Depression in the 1930s resulted in worldwide unemployment and poverty.

- In 1933 the Nazis gained power in Germany. Hitler rapidly removed all opposition.

- Stalin gained power in the Soviet Union. His main aims were rapid industrialisation and the collectivisation of agriculture.

- The Spanish Civil War ended with defeat of the Republicans by Franco's Nationalists.

- In the late 1930s the Fascist states began to invade foreign countries. The failure of the policy of appeasement led to World War II.

Activities

1. Look at Source A.

   a) Why do you think a map like this appeared in a German atlas in 1936?

   b) Has it any value for a study of German expansion from 1936? Give reasons for your answer.

2. a) Using Sources B and C write a defence of Chamberlain's policy of appeasement.

   b) Read Source D. What might a Czech have thought about Chamberlain's policy?

3. What does the cartoon in Source E tell us about British views of Hitler and Stalin?

A map of Europe in September 1939, just after the outbreak of the Second World War.

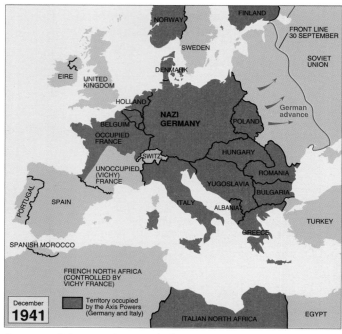

A map of Europe in December 1941. By then Italy had joined the war against Britain. France had been divided into two. The German army occupied the north and a pro-Nazi government based at the town of Vichy controlled the south. Germany attacked the Soviet Union in June 1941.

Themes

The first two years of the Second World War were a disaster for Britain and France. In May 1940 the German army swept through Belgium and Holland and defeated the British and French armies in northern France. By June Britain stood completely alone. A German invasion seemed inevitable.

In fact the invasion never came. Britain survived the Battle of Britain (a battle for air control, July to October 1940) and it survived the Blitz (the bombing of British towns, September 1940 to May 1941). By then Hitler had decided to invade the Soviet Union. German soldiers were moved to the east and the chance of invading Britain was lost.

This chapter looks at life in Britain during the war and asks the following questions.

- How was daily life affected by the war?
- Why did Winston Churchill become Prime Minister and what sort of leader was he?
- How did the British avoid invasion?

Focus Activities

1. You have been asked to design a museum exhibition on the theme, 'Britain goes to war'. Make a list of the exhibits you would use and explain why. Design a guide book for the exhibition.

2. What evidence is there in the Focus that preparations for war had already been made in Britain before 3 September 1939?

3. *Either:* If you know anyone who was alive in 1939, ask them what they did when war was declared and write a passage describing what they tell you.

   Or: Write a passage describing how you would have reacted to the news that Britain had declared war on Germany.

Great Britain at war

On 1 September 1939 Germany invaded Poland. Two days later Britain and France declared war on Germany. The Second World War had begun. The British government had been preparing for war for many months but how did people react to the news that war had actually been declared? The extracts on this page are taken from the diaries of Gwladys Cox and Joan Strange. Both were written in 1939.

The diary of Gwladys Cox who lived in North London during the war.

Sunday, 3 September 1939 We turned on the wireless (radio) and heard there was to be 'an important announcement' by the Prime Minister at 11.15 am. So, with bated breath, we settled ourselves in the sitting room and listened to Mr Chamberlain's broadcast. He announced that, as there had been no reply from the Germans by 11 am, we, as a nation, were at war with Germany. Mr Chamberlain's speech was followed by the playing of 'God Save the King' for which I rose and remained standing until it finished. Then, almost immediately, to our unspeakable astonishment, the air raid sirens sounded. Quickly turning off the gas at the main, catching Bob (the cat) and shutting him in his basket and grabbing our gas masks, we struggled down several flights of stairs to the street, some yards along the pavement, down the steps to our shelter. My knees were knocking together with weakness and I stifled a strong desire to be sick. We remained in the shelter for about half an hour. When the all clear sounded, we came upstairs to make preparations for Sunday dinner. Later we heard that the alert had been sounded for 'an unidentified aircraft'. I spent the rest of the day stripping the windows with gummed paper against bomb blast and improving the blackout (windows had to be blacked out to prevent German planes spotting built up areas at night).

The diary of Joan Strange who lived in Worthing, Sussex during the war.

Wednesday, 6 September 1939 The first week of war. It has been impossible to write daily for the last week because life has suddenly become very difficult under wartime conditions. Very few people felt that this terrible blow would fall and right up to Sunday morning (3 September) there was a glimmer of hope. On Friday the Germans 'crossed the frontiers to resist the Poles' and the newspapers immediately declared 'war begins'. Everyone's spirits sank but rose again when Mr Chamberlain gave Hitler one more chance in a message sent on Saturday with a time limit which ended at 11 am on Sunday morning. In the meantime the 'blackouts' have started, no one must show a glimmer of light anywhere. Some food especially sugar is very scarce. Ten thousand evacuees (people moved away from their homes to keep them safe) have been sent here from London and billeted on the locals (given a place to stay). We've had two air raid warnings already – one on Sunday morning at about 11.35 (20 minutes after the declaration of war) and one at 8.15 this morning. I must try to write this daily now but so far have not blacked out my bedroom windows. Blow! That's where I do my reading and writing.

The Phoney War

The Focus shows that, once war was declared, many people were worried and spent their time preparing for bombing raids or a German invasion. In fact they had little to be worried about (in terms of personal safety) for the next eight months. There was little fighting (once Poland had surrendered to Germany in September) and no bombs or an invasion. Because of this the period from September 1939 to May 1940 is known as the 'Phoney War'.

Although there was no direct threat to Britain during the Phoney War, the government encouraged people to prepare for the worst.

Source B   Government campaigns

Throughout the war the government produced posters like this one encouraging people to help with the war effort. In this campaign people were asked to grow their own food so that less food would need to be imported.

Source A   Bomb shelters and gas masks

This picture shows a family going in to their 'Anderson' shelter, a corrugated iron bomb shelter which was buried into the ground. Over 1 million shelters had been distributed to families before war was declared and another 1½ million were built over the next year. The family is carrying gas masks in boxes. The government encouraged people to carry gas masks with them wherever they went.

Source C   The blackout

'Well, it was your idea to have a black cat!'

From 1 September 1939 it became an offence to allow any light to be visible from outside a building at night. This was to prevent German bombers finding their targets. This cartoon makes a joke about the blackout. But it was no joke for some people. In East Ham in London, the number of road accidents at night tripled in September 1939 and HMV, a record company, had to pay £12,000 to get its factory blacked out.

In September 1939 children were evacuated (sent away) from cities that were likely to be bombed and went to live with families in the countryside. Although the government planned to move 3½ million children, only 1½ million left home. Many of the evacuated children came from poor backgrounds. The experience of evacuation could be exciting or difficult for both the children and their foster parents.

Source D   Before and during evacuation

Arriving at Gravesend for evacuation. Note the name tags and gas masks in boxes

Evacuees working on a farm

Source E

It was only 10 miles from Manchester but to us it was the country and a big adventure. Buses took us to a church hall. There we were looked over by the village people waiting to pick us out. Along with another girl, I was chosen by an older couple who took us to their home in a car. A car was something only 'well off' people had, so it was very exciting. They lived in a lovely large home with a garden front and back. The maid looked after us. I only remember once eating in the dining room with the family and I was never invited into the lounge. We had to be in early and used to look out at our friends still having fun on the swings. Parents just came up for the day.

Joan Giles who was evacuated on 1 September 1939 at the age of 12

Source F

Everything was so clean in the room. We were given flannels and toothbrushes. We'd never cleaned our teeth until then. And hot water came from the tap. And there was a lavatory upstairs. And carpets. And something called an eiderdown. This was all very odd. And rather scary.

Bernard Kops who was evacuated from Stepney in London in September 1939 at the age of 13

Activities

1. Look at Sources A, B and C.
   a) What do these sources tell us about the sort of dangers that the government expected Britain to face when war broke out?
   b) Write a diary which describes how life changed in Britain after war broke out.

2. Look at Sources D, E and F.
   a) What do the pictures in Source D tell us about evacuation.
   b) Suppose you were an evacuee. Write a letter to your parents explaining what happened to you during the Phoney War.
   c) Design a government poster encouraging parents to evacuate their children.

Winston Churchill

When the war broke out Neville Chamberlain remained Prime Minister even though he had supported the policy of 'appeasement' (giving in to demands in the hope that war could be avoided). As the Phoney War dragged on, however, Chamberlain lost more and more support. In early May 1940 MPs began to call for his resignation. The final straw came on May 10th. In the early hours of the morning the German army invaded Holland, Belgium and France. By the evening Chamberlain had resigned and Churchill was Prime Minister. To many people, Churchill seemed the obvious choice.

Source A The Churchill dynasty

Blenheim Palace today

Some historians talk of the Churchill 'dynasty'. Winston Churchill was born at Blenheim Palace which was given to his ancestor, the Duke of Marlborough (1650-1722), by Queen Anne after Marlborough had won the battle of Blenheim in 1704. Churchill wrote a biography of the Duke of Marlborough. He also wrote a biography of his father, Randolph (1849-95), a Conservative MP and later a Lord.

Source C Churchill's career

1874	Born
1888-92	Harrow school (a public school)
1893-95	Sandhurst Military Academy
1895-99	Soldier
1899	Journalist in South Africa
1900	Elected Conservative MP
1904	Joined the Liberal Party
1905-08	Junior minister
1908-15	Cabinet minister (held 4 different posts)
1917-22	Cabinet minister (held 3 different posts)
1922-24	Fails to be elected MP
1924	Returns to the Conservative Party and elected MP
1924-29	Cabinet minister (Chancellor of the Exchequer)
1929-39	MP on backbenches
1939-40	Cabinet minister
1940-45	Prime Minister
1945-51	Leader of the Opposition
1951-55	Prime Minister
1955-65	Retirement until death

Source B Churchill and the Boer War

> **£25**
> (Twenty-five Pounds stg.) REWARD is offered by the Sub-Commission of the fifth division, on behalf of the Special Constable of the said division, to anyone who brings the escaped prisoner of war
> **CHURCHILL,**
> dead or alive to this office.
> For the Sub-Commission of the fifth division.
> (Signed) LODK. de HAAS, Sec.

A reward offered for Churchill's capture, dead or alive, after his escape during the Boer War in South Africa

Churchill during his election campaign 1900

Winston Churchill first came into the public eye in 1899. At the beginning of the year he failed to get elected as an MP. But when the Boer War broke out a few months later, he went to South Africa as a journalist. Soon afterwards he was captured but managed to escape. His story was published in the newspapers and, on his return, he had no trouble gaining election as an MP.

Source D The Sidney Street Siege

In 1911 three armed men who had killed three police officers during a burglary were surrounded by the police in a house in Sidney Street, London. Churchill, then Home Secretary (Cabinet minister in charge of law and order), hurried there. When the house caught fire, it was allowed to burn down and two of the men were found dead. Opponents criticised Churchill for going to the scene, which was risky, and taking over the operation.

Source E Churchill in World War I

On 20 May 1915 Winston Churchill was dismissed from his post as First Lord of the Admiralty (in charge of the navy). He was blamed by the Conservatives for a naval defeat in Turkey.

'I am finished!'

'Not finished at forty with your remarkable powers!'

'Yes. Finished in respect of all I care for – the waging of war; the defeat of the Germans. I have had a high place offered to me (a non-military post). But all that goes for nothing. This is what I live for.'

Conversation with Sir George Riddell, 20 May 1915

Source F Churchill speech 1934

I dread the day when the means of threatening the heart of the British Empire should pass into the hands of the present rulers of Germany (the Nazis). That day is not, perhaps, far distant.

Part of a speech made by Churchill in 1934

Source G The 'wilderness years'

A painting of the French Riviera by Churchill

The years 1929 to 1939 have been described as Churchill's 'wilderness years'. Although he had held eight posts in the Cabinet before 1929, he was not offered another post until 1939. During this time Churchill was one of the few MPs to argue that the Nazis were preparing for war and were a great threat to Britain. He made many speeches and wrote many articles pleading with the government to rearm before it was too late. At first he was described as a scaremonger and few people listened to him. But by 1939 his predictions seemed to have been correct. During the 'wilderness years' Churchill spent much of his spare time painting.

Activities

1. What do Sources A and C tell us about Churchill's background and career?

2. Churchill's supporters described him as 'a man of action'. His opponents described him as 'reckless'. Find evidence to support both views in Sources B and D.

3. What does Source E tell us about Churchill's personality?

4. Look at Sources F and G. Why have 1929-39 been described as Churchill's 'wilderness years'? Why might they have helped his career? Explain your answer.

5. Using Sources A to G, write a short article entitled 'Winston Churchill – his career and personality 1874-1939'.

Winston Churchill PM

During his 'wilderness years' Churchill had warned time and again of the threat of a Nazi invasion. As soon as he became Prime Minister that threat seemed very real. The German advance on 10 May 1940 was immediately successful. Within two weeks the British and French armies had been pushed back to the English Channel and there was a great danger that they would be captured or killed.

Because Churchill became Prime Minister at a time of crisis and remained in office until victory had been won, he has often been praised for his leadership. But what sort of leader was he?

Source B

At my request, Mr Attlee (leader of the Labour Party) called upon me. I asked if Labour would join the government. He said they would. I had of course known Atlee for a long time. During the 10 years before the outbreak of war I had (because of my independent position) come far more often into collision with my own Party, the Conservatives, than with the Labour and Liberal Parties.

Winston Churchill's memoirs published in 1948

Source D   British cartoon, 1940

Even before war was declared there had been a poster campaign demanding that Churchill be made Prime Minister. When he was finally appointed, he was a popular choice. This cartoon shows members of all political parties and the general public in support of Churchill. Even the ex-Prime Minister, Chamberlain, is shown marching with him.

Source A   Churchill's War Cabinet

The members of Chamberlain's War Cabinet had all come from the Conservative Party. As soon as he was appointed, Churchill asked members of the Labour Party to join his Cabinet. In this picture, Clement Attlee, leader of the Labour Party (front row, second from the right) sits next to Churchill (second from the left).

Source C

You ask, what is our policy? It is to wage war by sea, land and air, with all our might and with all the strength that God can give us, to wage war against a monstrous tyranny. That is our policy. You ask, what is our aim? I can answer in one word: victory. Victory at all costs. Victory in spite of all terror. Victory, however long and hard the road may be. For, without victory there is no survival. Let that be understood. No survival for the British Empire. No survival for all that the British Empire has stood for. But I take up my task with buoyancy and hope. I feel sure that our cause will not fail. At this time I feel entitled to claim the aid of all and I say, 'Come then, let us go forward together with our united strength'.

Speech made by Churchill in the House of Commons on 13 May, 1940

This is the first of many speeches made on this theme. Churchill often repeated speeches made in the House of Commons later in the day on the radio. At that time speeches made in the House of Commons were not broadcast.

Source E   The evacuation from Dunkirk, northern France

When it became clear that it would be impossible to defend France, Churchill made the decision to evacuate as many soldiers as possible. This was a desperate measure. Between 24 May and 3 June 1940 over 200,000 British and over 100,000 French soldiers were evacuated from the beaches of Dunkirk. A vast fleet of boats sailed day and night between Britain and France to carry the soldiers to safety (often under fire). Churchill admitted on 4 June that he had feared no more than 30,000 troops would be saved and he would have to announce 'the greatest military disaster in our history'.

Source F   Churchill and the USA

HOLDING THE LINE

As soon as he became Prime Minister, Churchill sent messages to the American President, Roosevelt, asking for aid and encouraging him to join the war. In the USA there was concern about the future of democracy and support for Churchill grew. This poster was produced in America in 1940. It shows Churchill as the British Bulldog holding the line against the Nazi advance.

Source G   Churchill under pressure

My darling,

I hope you will forgive me if I tell you something you ought to know. One of the men on your staff (a devoted friend) has told me that there is a danger of you being disliked by your colleagues because of your rough, sarcastic and overbearing manner. It seems that your Private Secretaries have agreed to behave like school boys by 'taking what's coming to them' and then escaping. Higher up, if any idea is suggested (say at a conference) you are so quick to reject it that soon no ideas, good or bad, will be suggested. I was upset to hear this and was told, 'No doubt it's the strain'. I cannot bear it that those who serve the country and yourself should not love you. Besides you won't get the best results by anger and rudeness. They will breed either dislike or a slave mentality. Please forgive your loving, devoted and watchful wife, Clemmie.

Letter from Clementine Churchill to her husband, June 1940

Activities

1. Look at Sources A and B. Why did Churchill want the Labour Party to join the government?

2. 'Churchill in public was very different from Churchill in private.' Explain this statement using Sources C and G. What do the two sources tell us about Churchill's leadership qualities?

3. What do the pictures in Sources D and F tell us about what the public at home and in the USA thought of Churchill? How might the German view have been different?

4. You are a British soldier on the beach at Dunkirk on 25 May 1940. Using Source E describe what happened during the evacuation.

The Battle of Britain

One week after the evacuation from Dunkirk Italy joined the war on the side of the Germans. A week later France surrendered. Britain now stood alone. Hitler waited for the British to seek peace. But Parliament fully supported Churchill's determination to fight to the end. Therefore, Hitler ordered his commanders to prepare for invasion. The first phase was to gain air control. This would make invasion by land much easier. The result was the Battle of Britain – an air battle between the Luftwaffe (German air force) and the RAF from 10 July to 31 October 1940. The Luftwaffe had been successful in the advance through France and expected an easy victory. But the Luftwaffe was unable to destroy the British air force. In early September Hitler decided that daylight raids were too costly. Britain had managed to win its first victory in the war.

Source A

What General Weygand (the French Commander) called the 'Battle of France' is over. I expect that the Battle of Britain is about to begin. The whole fury and might of the enemy must very soon be turned on us. Let us therefore be prepared to do our duty so that, if the British Empire lasts for a thousand years, men will say, 'This was their finest hour'.

Radio broadcast by Winston Churchill, 18 June 1940

The British have lost the war but they don't know it. One must give them time and they will come round.

Adolf Hitler, June 1940

Source B   WAAFs and the Battle of Britain

Although all RAF pilots were men, there were 8,000 women in the Women's Auxiliary Air Force (WAAF). This picture shows WAAFs raising a barrage balloon. These balloons prevented German planes flying low.

Source C   A 'dogfight'

There's one coming down in flames – someone's hit a German and he's coming down – there's a long streak – he's coming down completely out of control – a long streak of smoke – ah, the man's baled out by parachute – the pilot's baled out by parachute and he's going slap into the sea and there he goes sma-a-ash. Oh boy, I've never seen anything as good as this. The RAF fighters have really got these boys taped.

Charles Gardner's live BBC radio description of a 'dogfight' (a fight between two planes) over Kent, 10 July 1940

Source D   The balance of forces

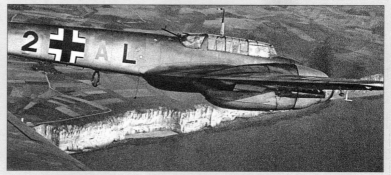

A German plane approaching Britain. At the beginning of the Battle of Britain the Luftwaffe had 2,670 planes whilst the RAF had only 600. Despite this, by careful planning and tactics, the RAF was able to shoot down enough German planes to give the impression that it was not worthwhile for the Germans to continue daytime raids.

Source E   Radar - an early warning system

I was one of the first WAAFs to train as a radar operator. At 1 pm on 18 August 1940 our screens showed a big raid building up over France. Sergeant Blundell ordered me over to the bomb-proof building. No sooner had I sat down than he rang through telling me to 'duck' as raiders were approaching. I told him I couldn't leave my post as so much information was coming in. He said, 'I'll leave it to you'. Bombs were already falling on the station and I could hear the scream of the dive bombers as they swooped down. The next thing I knew was that the door had blown in and dust was flying everywhere. Outside there was devastation. I was told that the Germans had dropped about eighty 500lb bombs.

Corporal Avis Hearn quoted in Vera Lynn, 'Unsung Heroines', 1990

A radar station. Radar gave the RAF early warning of a German attack. A network of stations covered Britain. Even when one station had been bombed, other stations continued to work while it was repaired. This gave the impression that bombing them had little effect.

Source F   The impact of the Battle of Britain

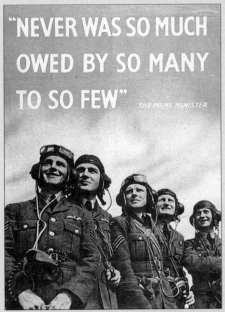

The poster on the left includes a famous line from a speech made by Churchill on 20 August 1940. The poster on the right advertises a film released in 1942.

Activities

1. What does Source A tell us about the mood of the British and German governments in June 1940?

2. Using Sources B and E describe the part played by women in the Battle of Britain.

3. Using Sources C, D and E explain the RAF's success. Why was it so important for Britain to win?

4. Look at Source F. Why do you think that the Battle of Britain was used as the theme for posters and films later in the war?

The Blitz

In July 1940 Hitler had forbidden the bombing of cities because he feared that the British would retaliate by bombing German cities. But on 24 August 1940 German bombers missed a military target and dropped their bombs on London. The next night Churchill ordered 81 bombers to bomb Berlin. This successful raid on Berlin proved that the Luftwaffe had failed to destroy the RAF and win control of the air.

Two weeks later Hitler decided to change tactics. The Luftwaffe was now ordered to bomb cities by night rather than to fight British planes by day. Each night from 7 September to mid May 1941 German bombers dropped bombs on British cities. This is known as the 'Blitz' (Blitzkrieg is German for 'lightning war'). In London 10,000 people were killed and over 1.5 million houses were damaged or destroyed. But it was not only London which suffered. From October other cities were bombed. On 14 November, for example, 437 German bombers dropped over 600 tons of bombs on Coventry. The city centre was destroyed and over 500 people died.

Source A   Bomb damage

A London street the day after a bombing raid. London was the main target of raids throughout the Blitz. It was Britain's largest city and easy to locate because the River Thames could be seen at night.

Source B   An Italian comment on the Blitz

An Italian poster produced in 1940. Londra means London. In ancient Rome at gladiatorial combats the Emperor decided whether or not a defeated gladiator should survive. If he turned his thumb down, it meant that the gladiator should die.

Source C   Hitler's view

The British drop bombs on civilian houses, farms and villages. I did not reply because I believed that they would stop. Mr Churchill took this as a sign of weakness. The British will know that we are giving our answer. If they attack our cities, we will simply erase theirs. We shall stop the handiwork of those night pirates, so help us God.

Radio broadcast made by Adolf Hitler on 4 September 1940

Source D   Churchill's view

These cruel bombings of London are, of course, part of Hitler's invasion plans. He hopes, by killing large numbers of women and children, that he will terrorise and break the spirit of the people of this mighty city. Little does he know the spirit of the British nation or the tough fibre of the Londoners who have been bred to value freedom far above their lives. This wicked man has now decided to try to break our famous Island race by slaughter and destruction. What he has done is to kindle a fire in British hearts, here and all over the world, which will glow long after all traces of the blaze he has caused in London have been removed. He has lit a fire which will burn until the last traces of Nazi tyranny have been burnt out of Europe.

Radio broadcast made by Winston Churchill on 11 September 1940

Source E   A cartoon drawn during the Blitz

'Oh, Mr Butterfield, Mr Fitzsimmonds would like to see you in his office at once'

This cartoon appeared in the magazine 'Punch' on 12 February 1941.

Source F   Sheltering below ground

This picture shows people sheltering in a Tube station during the Blitz. Many people preferred to sleep there rather than in cramped Anderson shelters (though a survey taken in November 1940 showed that, surprisingly, only 40% of Londoners regularly went to any shelter during a raid). At the beginning of the war the government had rejected the use of Tube stations for shelter. But people simply bought a ticket and stayed down there. By late September 1940 the government had given in to public demand. Some 80 stations sheltered 177,000 people each night. All types of people sheltered together and often entertainment was provided.

Activities

1. Using Sources A, E, F and G describe how the Blitz affected normal life in British cities. Some people say that the Blitz 'brought out the best in people'. Suggest reasons for this.

2. What does the poster in Source B show? Why do you think it was produced? Draw a poster from the British point of view.

3. What reasons did Hitler give for bombing British cities in Source C? Do you think they were the real reasons?

4. Suppose you had just listened to Churchill's broadcast in Source D. Describe your reaction to it.

5. Compare Sources C and D. What do they tell us about the leadership style of Hitler and Churchill? In what ways are they similar? In what ways are they different?

Source G   London hotel is hit

There was an air raid alert. I wondered whether I should go to the underground shelter but decided I was too tired and that it would probably be only a few bombs on the docks as usual. I went back to the lounge and there were long minutes of silence. And then it happened. The air shook with volcanic rumbling and a marble pillar in the centre of the room cracked like a tree trunk. In the chaos – dust, tumbling masonry and splintering woodwork – people were screaming. I may have screamed too, I don't know. The walls seemed to burst apart. The centre of the floor shattered and the debris thundered down into the basement. There was one terrible cry from the shelterers below. Suddenly I realised that I should be helping people, not just standing there frozen with horror.

The diary of Mary Mulrey, 11 May 1941

Pulling through

The Blitz ended in mid May 1941 because Hitler had decided to invade the Soviet Union and moved most of his troops to the eastern front. Although there were some air raids after this, there was nothing to compare with the scale of the Blitz until new V1 bombs began to be dropped in 1944. The end of the Blitz meant that for the first time since the beginning of the war a German invasion seemed unlikely. In addition Hitler's invasion of the Soviet Union meant that Britain was no longer isolated. In July 1941 Britain and the Soviet Union became allies. Six months later the USA joined the alliance. By winning the Battle of Britain and hanging on during the Blitz, Britain won time to regain strength and, eventually, to defeat the Nazis.

Source B   Entertainment

The Entertainment National Service Association (ENSA) was set up in August 1939 to entertain British troops at home and abroad. At first it earned the nickname 'Every Night Something Awful' but it soon improved. From 1940 ENSA also entertained people sheltering during the Blitz and shows were performed in the workplace. During the war four fifths of British entertainers appeared for ENSA and its total audience was several million.

Source A   Rationing

In January 1940 the government introduced rationing. Every family was given a book of stamps which could be exchanged for a fixed amount of certain goods. At first only butter, sugar and bacon were rationed. But as it became more difficult to import goods, more were rationed (for example, clothes and petrol). This picture shows the weekly ration for two people in 1941 (bread and other goods which were not rationed are not shown). Some families (especially the very poor) had never eaten so well or had such a balanced diet.

Source C   Doodlebugs

By 1944 the Germans had invented new bombs which could be launched from overseas. The V1 (also known as the 'doodlebug' or 'buzz bomb') was a flying bomb – a small, pilotless plane carrying a 1 ton bomb which dropped and exploded when it ran out of fuel. Later in the year V2s – missiles with rocket motors which had a longer range and greater impact – were launched.

I was standing at the window while a buzz bomb's sound came towards us. Across the road, two women were coming out of the greengrocer's deep in gossip. The young blind girl who walked down the street twice every day was rattling her stick around the hole from which a workman was emerging and a young man had just crossed the road. At that moment the buzz bomb cut out. The two women, still talking, stepped back into the greengrocer's; the workman slid back down the hole; the young man took the arm of the blind girl pulling her with him into the nearest doorway. There was a 'swoosh' and an explosion nearby and everyone moved again. The women, still talking, came out of the shop; the workman reappeared; the blind girl nodded to the young man who raised his hat and they all continued on their way.

Megan Ryan, July 1944

Source D   Americans in Britain

When the USA joined the war American soldiers were brought over to Britain so that they could be transported to Europe easily. Few Americans had visited Britain. The following extracts are from a pamphlet given to the first American troops to arrive in Britain in January 1942.

British and American people are very much alike but each country has minor national differences. For instance, the British are often more reserved than we are. So if Britons don't strike up conversation with you, it doesn't mean they're being unfriendly. Also the British have words and phrases which may sound funny to you. It isn't a good idea, for instance, to say 'bloody' in mixed company – it's one of their worst swear words. If Britain looks a little grimy to you, remember that you're not seeing the country at its best. The houses haven't been painted because the factories are not making paint – they're making planes. The British are enthusiastic about sports. Cricket will strike you as slow compared to baseball.

Some Important Dos and Don'ts
Be friendly but don't intrude. If you're invited to eat with a family, don't eat too much or you may eat up the weekly rations. Don't try to tell the British that America won the last war. Never criticise the King or Queen.

'A Short Guide To Britain', January 1942

Source E   British propaganda

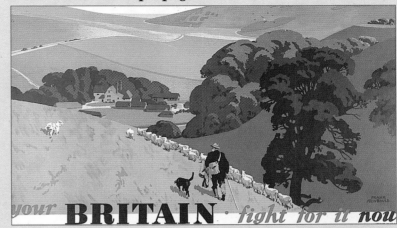

Both these posters were produced for the government but the bottom one was banned by the government censor.

Checklist

- In Britain the first 18 months of the war were dominated by fear of a German invasion.
- Victory in the Battle of Britain forced Hitler to postpone his planned invasion. Despite the great destruction caused by the Blitz, people's spirits remained high.
- Although there was little threat of invasion after May 1941, daily life continued to be disrupted by the war.

Activities

1. 'During the war, everyone was equal and there was a community spirit.' Use Sources A, B and C to explain this statement.

2. How useful do you think the pamphlet in Source D would be to American troops?

Explain your answer.

3. Look at Source E. Why do you think the bottom poster was banned but the top one was not? What does this tell us about the way Britain was governed during the war?

5 BRITAIN'S ALLIES

A Nazi cartoon from occupied Belgium. Churchill and Stalin are on the left, Roosevelt on the right. 'Entente cordiale' means friendly agreement.

Themes

In 1941 two events occurred which changed the course of World War II. In June 1941 the German army invaded the Soviet Union. By breaking the Nazi-Soviet pact of 1939 without warning, Hitler hoped that his army would take the Soviet Union by surprise and win a quick victory. In fact the Soviet people managed to resist the German advance and, by moving his troops to the east, Hitler gave Britain a breathing space.

Then, in December 1941, the Japanese air force attacked the American naval base at Pearl Harbour. This brought the USA into the war. Japan's allies, Germany and Italy, declared war on the USA. The USA therefore joined the war in Europe as well as fighting against Japan in Asia.

At the beginning of 1941 Britain fought alone. By the end of the year two new allies had joined the war on Britain's side – the Soviet Union and the USA. It was from this point that the war truly become a world war.

This chapter looks at the following questions.

- Why did the Soviet Union and the USA join the war on Britain's side?
- What part did these countries play in the war?
- What sort of leadership did Stalin and Roosevelt provide during the war?

A Soviet cartoon. Mussolini is on the left, Hitler on the right.

Focus Activities

1. a) What does the Focus tell us about Britain's relations with its allies?

    b) Would you say that the evidence in the Focus is reliable? Explain your answer.

2. Why were the meetings of the Big Three so important?

3. Describe what each of the cartoons on this page shows.

The Big Three

Stalin (leader of the Soviet Union), Roosevelt (President of the USA) and Churchill (Prime Minister of Britain) meet in Tehran, December 1943.

The need to defeat a common enemy brought the three Allied leaders (the Big Three) together. Their meetings were vital because they resulted in agreements about the best way to fight the war. But the Big Three did not always agree, especially about what was to happen at the end of the war. There was a long history of suspicion between Communist and non-Communist countries. The passages below show what Winston Churchill thought of the other two members of the Alliance, Stalin and Roosevelt.

Letter from Churchill to Roosevelt, 6 September 1940

I did not think it right for me as a foreigner to make public my opinion about American politics while the election for President was on, but now I feel you will not mind my saying that I prayed for your success and I am truly thankful for it. We are entering a difficult phase in the war and I look forward to being able to exchange my thoughts with you in all that confidence and goodwill which has grown up between us since the war started.

Washington DC, 1941

I landed after dark on 22 December 1941 at Washington airport. President Roosevelt was waiting for me there in his car. I grasped his strong hand with comfort and pleasure. I had formed a very strong affection for him. This grew with our years of comradeship.

Moscow, 1942

I had once seen the Soviet Union as the enemy of civilised freedom and knew that, until the Germans attacked them, the Soviets would have watched the Germans sweep us out of existence without a care. Still, I was sure that it was my duty to have it out with Stalin face to face. At least it showed that I cared and understood what their struggle meant to the war in general. So now, for the first time, I met Stalin, the great revolutionary chief and warrior. Over the next three years I was to have a close, rigorous but always exciting and, at times, even friendly relationship with him.

At one point in our conversation Stalin was glum and restless and said his view of the war was different from mine. I told him we had done our utmost to help the Soviet Union and would continue to do so. Now that the three great nations were allied, victory was certain so long as we did not fall apart. The conversation began again in a less tense atmosphere.

Tehran, 1943

Since I knew that Roosevelt and Stalin had held a private meeting, I suggested that Roosevelt and I might have lunch together. Roosevelt said no and explained that he did not want Stalin to know that he and I were meeting privately. I felt that Stalin was not getting a true impression of the British position.

I hosted the dinner on my 69th birthday. Everything passed off agreeably. Stalin and Roosevelt beamed with pleasure. On my right sat the President of the USA, on my left the master of the Soviet Union. Between us we controlled a large proportion of the armed forces of the world. We had come a long way on the road to victory since 1940 when Britain stood alone.

Extracts from Churchill's memoirs, 1951

The Soviet Union: the path to war

The rise to power of Mussolini and Hitler meant one party rule in Italy and Germany. The two leaders ruled as dictators. They imprisoned or murdered opponents and used propaganda to build up their image as strong leaders. In the late 1930s Stalin began to use the same techniques in the Soviet Union.

In the early 1930s there had been opposition to Stalin, especially over the forced collectivisation of farms (see page 27), but by 1936 his power seemed greater than ever. Despite this, Stalin decided to remove all possible rivals and opponents. The result was the 'great purges' of 1936-38. Those whom Stalin saw as rivals were put on trial in public ('show trials'), forced to confess that they had acted as 'enemies of the state' and then executed. Anyone suspected of being an opponent was arrested and sent to the 'gulags' (prison camps). Historians estimate that between 12 and 20 million people suffered this fate. As the purges were taking place Stalin began a massive propaganda campaign to build up his image as a leader.

The great purges took place at a time when the threat of war was growing and they had a serious effect on Soviet preparations for war. Stalin tried to buy time by reaching an agreement with his most hated opponent, Hitler (see page 33). Although it suited Hitler to make an alliance with Stalin in 1939, invasion of the Soviet Union still remained Hitler's long term goal.

Source A   Show trials

In late spring 1936 a series of arrests of Nazi spies (the first people to be put on trial in public) revealed the existence of an organisation which had close ties with the German secret police.

A. Rothstein, 'A History of the USSR', 1950

The Commission (set up to investigate the purges) has proved that many of the people described in 1936-38 as 'enemies' were never enemies or spies but were actually honest Communists. Often they charged themselves with all sorts of serious and unlikely crimes because they were no longer able to bear barbaric tortures.

N. Khrushchev's 'Secret Speech' made to Communist leaders in 1956, three years after Stalin's death

Source B   Propaganda

'Day and night the radio told us that Stalin was the greatest man on earth.' This picture, taken in 1937, shows a portrait of Stalin with Lenin in the background on the wall of a ball bearing factory.

Source C   British cartoon drawn in 1936

" IT'S QUEER HOW YOU REMIND ME OF SOMEONE, JOSEF . . ."

When news of the show trials reached Britain, it confirmed many people's fear of Communism. It made the British government less likely to see Stalin as an ally against Nazism.

Source D

Gradually Stalin became a virtual deity (god). No Russian town was without its Stalin Square or Avenue and its Stalin statue. Poets and musicians wrote works in praise of him. The top prize for literature was the Stalin prize. The worship was undoubtedly fixed but in many hearts it was sincere.

R. Cornwall, 'The Independent', 1987

Source E   Military power

There was a race to build faster aircraft and more powerful tanks. But the Soviet arms industry could not change swiftly. Of 24,000 Soviet tanks operational in June 1941, only 946 were as good as German tanks at that time. On top of this came the purges – 90% of all generals and 80% of all colonels were victims. This included many who had the most up to date military ideas.

P. Kennedy, 'The Rise and Fall of the Great Powers', 1988

Source F   Soviet victory against Japan, 1939

Encouraged by stories of Soviet military weakness resulting from the purges, Japan attacked the Soviet Union in April 1939. This picture shows newly designed Soviet T-34 tanks which played an important part in the defeat of the Japanese at the Battle of Nomonhan (August 1939). 18,000 Japanese soldiers were killed and the Soviet Union removed the danger of war with Japan.

Source G   The Nazi-Soviet pact, 1939

WONDER HOW LONG THE HONEYMOON WILL LAST?

An American cartoon showing the 'marriage' of Hitler and Stalin. Stalin justified the treaty with Germany for the following reasons:

1. **Britain and France had offered no support and clearly did not mind if Hitler attacked the Soviet Union.**
2. **It bought time to build up arms.**
3. **A secret agreement was made giving the Soviet Union territory which provided a defensive barrier against Germany.**

Source H   Hitler breaks the pact

Anxious to avoid war, Stalin ignored warnings from British and Soviet spies that the Germans were preparing to invade in June 1941.

Despite the absurdity of these rumours of invasion by Germany, the government has thought it necessary to state that the rumours are put out by forces hostile to the Soviet Union and Germany.

Statement from the official Soviet news agency, 'Tass', broadcast nine days before the German invasion of the Soviet Union, June 1941

Activities

1. Look at Sources A, B, C and D. What signs are there that Stalin ruled as a dictator?
2. What do Sources A and E tell us about the Great Purges?
3. Look at Sources E, F and G. What do they tell us about Soviet military strength in 1939?
4. Look at Sources G and H. Would you say that Stalin was right to make the Nazi-Soviet pact?
5. Using the sources on these pages explain why Britain was reluctant to have a close relationship with the Soviet Union before 1941.

The eastern front

By the time that the news of the German invasion was announced to the Soviet people, the German army was 100 miles inside the territory that the Soviet Union had gained as a result of the Nazi-Soviet pact. The first feelings of shock at the suddenness and speed of the German attack later gave way to a spirit of grim resistance. Stalin recalled the invasion by Napoleon in 1812 and his eventual defeat. This was to be another 'Great Patriotic War'. The losses in people and materials were enormous but in 1943 the Germans were forced to retreat.

Source B   Stalin's reactions

Stalin was in collapse, thinking this was the end. 'All that Lenin created we have lost', he said. Stalin ceased to do anything at all.

N. Khrushchev (Stalin's successor), 'Memoirs', 1971

Our government has made not a few mistakes. There were moments of desperation in 1941 and 1942. Another nation might have told me to get out. But the Russian people did not. Thank you, great Russian people, for this trust.

Stalin, speech made in May 1945

Source D   The siege of Leningrad

While one section of Hitler's army advanced towards Moscow, another aimed to capture Leningrad. The city was besieged from September 1941 to January 1944. According to H. Salisbury, 'More people died in the Leningrad siege than ever died in a modern city anywhere, any time.' Estimates vary between 1 and 1.5 million. Of these, probably over 600,000 died of starvation. This picture shows people leaving their homes which have been destroyed by Nazi bombs.

Source A   Operation Barbarossa

The Nazis called the invasion of the Soviet Union in June 1941 'Operation Barbarossa'. It was the biggest military operation ever mounted.

Source C

Pulling a body through the streets of Leningrad

Source E

Faces in the street are drawn and shiny – or green and lumpy. The skeletons are being gnawed by frost. As I write these words I can hear a mouse, crazy with hunger, rummaging in the wastepaper basket, into which we used to throw crumbs. It hasn't even the strength to rejoice that all the cats have been eaten.

Diary kept by a woman in Leningrad, 1942

Source F   Moscow and Stalingrad

In December 1941 the German advance was stopped only 20 miles from their greatest prize – the Soviet capital, Moscow. Their other major military target, further south, was Stalingrad. In September 1942, after bitter street fighting, the Germans took control of most of the city only to find themselves cut off and besieged. This picture shows German soldiers in Stalingrad. In February 1943 they surrendered. The Soviets took over 100,000 prisoners. 70,000 Germans died during the siege. It was a turning point in the war.

Source G   The eastern front 1942-44

Legend:
- Soviet-German frontier October 1939
- Front line November 1942
- Soviet gains to April 1943
- Retaken by Germans June - July 1943
- Soviet gains July 1943 - April 1944
- German occupied territory April 1944
- Soviet advance

Hitler needed a quick victory. The Soviet Union had the resources (both people and materials) to defeat Germany if the Soviet army could hold out. Between June and October 1942, for example, the Soviets produced 900 tanks, 1,300 big guns and 11,000 planes. This map shows the great turn around that occurred on the eastern front between 1942 and 1944.

Activities

1. Using the maps in Sources A and G write an article for a German newspaper which explains what happened:

   a) between June and December 1941

   b) between 1942 and 1944.

2. a) What do Sources B and I tell us about Stalin's leadership in the war?

   b) Stalin never admitted he 'collapsed' in June 1941. Does Source B prove that he did?

3. Suppose you had been a Russian who survived the siege of Leningrad. Use Sources C, D and E to describe what happened.

4. Use Sources F, G and H to explain why the Germans failed to defeat the Soviet Union.

Source H   German defeat

The icy cold (–40°C, oil in German tanks froze), the lack of shelter, the shortage of clothing, the heavy losses of men and equipment and the wretched state of our fuel supplies were the things that led to our defeat.

General Gudarian, the German tank commander in the Soviet Union, speaking after the German defeat

Source I   Stalin and his generals

Russian commanders were men who had proved themselves so able that they could insist on doing things their own way.

Comment made by a German general after the war

Stalin had the sense to give back to his generals their freedom of movement.

I. Deutscher, 'Stalin', 1961

The war taught Stalin a great deal. He has understood that he can be mistaken and that the experience and knowledge of others can be valuable.

Marshal Voroshilov, a Soviet commander speaking after the war

The USA: the path to war

Many Americans in the 1930s saw no reason to get involved in the war in Europe. They felt that the USA had enough problems of its own with the Great Depression.

Between 1935 and 1937 Congress (the American Parliament) passed the Neutrality Laws to try to keep the USA out of wars. But President Roosevelt became alarmed at Germany's successes in 1940-41 and persuaded Congress to pass the Lend Lease Law. This allowed Britain to 'borrow' military equipment without cash payment.

The USA did not only feel threatened by the war in Europe. In the 1930s Japan's government was controlled by army commanders. They planned to create a Japanese Empire in East Asia. In 1932 the army invaded Manchuria (see page 30). Then between 1937 and 1939 Japan fought in China and the Soviet Union. The USA saw Japanese expansion as a threat because it interfered with American trade in the Pacific.

In September 1940 Japan, Germany and Italy made a pact to support each other. Japan became an Axis power. The USA imposed sanctions on Japan in the hope that this would persuade Japan to keep the peace. Instead the sanctions convinced Japanese leaders that the USA would oppose any attempt to build a Japanese Empire. As a result they planned a surprise attack on the USA. They hoped that this would give them time to gain control of East Asia.

Source A   The New Deal

A cartoon illustrating the New Deal

When Roosevelt became President in 1933, unemployment in the USA had reached nearly 13 million, 25% of the workforce. He promised a New Deal to cure America's economic ills. Measures were taken to boost American business and the Social Security Act of 1935 provided pensions and unemployment benefit. A social worker said about these measures, 'More progress was made in public welfare in 10 years than in the previous 100 years'.

Source B   The Neutrality Laws (1935-37)

1. Americans were forbidden to sell arms to countries at war.
2. Such countries were only allowed to buy non-military materials if they paid cash and collected them in their own ships (the 'Cash and Carry' Laws).
3. No American loans were to be made to countries at war.
4. No American citizens were to travel on ships belonging to countries at war.

Source C   A British cartoon, 1941

A British cartoonist's view of Lend Lease

Source D   The Lend Lease Law (March 1941)

Suppose my neighbour's house catches fire and I have a length of garden hose 500 feet away. If he can take the hose and connect it up, I may help him to put out the fire. I don't say to him, 'Neighbour, my garden hose cost $15. You have to pay me $15 for it.' I don't want $15, I just want my hose back after the fire is over.

Roosevelt explaining Lend Lease, December 1940

Source E — American cartoon, 1940

Uncle Sam (the USA) and John Bull (Britain) pleading in chains in front of Hitler (and other Nazis), Mussolini (holding the fan) and a Japanese soldier.

Source F — A warning

If we go down you may have a United States of Europe under Nazi command which is far stronger and far better armed than the USA. It has now become most urgent for you to let us have warships, motor boats, aircraft and ammunition.

Churchill's warning to Roosevelt in a letter written in 1940

Source G — Opposition to Roosevelt

TO THE DELEGATES TO THE REPUBLICAN NATIONAL CONVENTION AND TO AMERICAN MOTHERS, WAGE EARNERS, FARMERS AND VETERANS

STOP THE MARCH TO WAR!
STOP THE INTERVENTIONISTS AND WARMONGERS!
STOP THE DEMOCRATIC PARTY

WHICH, WE BELIEVE, IS THE WAR PARTY IN THE UNITED STATES, AND IS LEADING US TO WAR AGAINST THE WILL OF THE AMERICAN PEOPLE!

THE NATIONAL COMMITTEE TO KEEP AMERICA OUT OF FOREIGN WARS

Source H — Churchill meets Roosevelt

In August 1941 Churchill and Roosevelt met on board a ship off the coast of Canada. They agreed common aims for the war, even though the USA had not yet entered it. They also outlined their hopes for the world after the defeat of the Nazis – peace and security for all nations and the right to hold free elections.

Activities

1. What does the cartoonist in Source A think about Roosevelt's New Deal?

2. How do you think the Neutrality Laws in Source B were meant to keep the USA out of war?

3. Look at Sources C and D.
   a) How was Lend Lease intended to work?
   b) What point is the cartoonist making about Lend Lease?

4. Look at Sources C–H.
   a) What evidence is there to suggest Roosevelt was under pressure to join the war on Britain's side?
   b) What were the arguments for joining the war?
   c) Why do you think some people opposed America's entry into the war?

The USA at war

Early on 7 December 1941, 353 Japanese planes, launched from 6 aircraft carriers, attacked the American naval base at Pearl Harbour on Oahu, one of the Hawaiian Islands in the Pacific Ocean. The raid destroyed 6 battleships, 3 cruisers, 3 destroyers and 149 planes. Over 4,000 American soldiers and civilians were killed or wounded. The American Pacific fleet was caught completely by surprise. The following day the USA declared war on Japan. Three days later Germany and Italy declared war on the USA. This brought the USA into the war in Europe.

Source B

Before me lay the whole American Pacific fleet in a formation I would not have dreamed of, anchored at a distance of 500 to 1,000 yards apart. A war fleet must always be on the alert against a surprise attack. The Americans were not alert. This was difficult to understand.

A Japanese bomber pilot who attacked the American fleet at Pearl Harbour

Source C   American cartoon, December 1941

The cover of an American magazine published five days after the attack on Pearl Harbour.

Source A   Pearl Harbour, December 1941

An American warship is destroyed at Pearl Harbour.

Source D   Why were the Americans caught by surprise?

The American government knew that Japan was likely to attack. They could intercept Japanese messages because they had broken the Japanese code. A dispatch rider carrying a warning of the attack sheltered in a ditch as the bombers came over. His message could have been sent directly and earlier. What happened? There are two views.

1. There was a mixture of confusion and neglect. Indications of the attack were not taken seriously enough because, at heart, the Americans simply did not believe that the Japanese would dare to attack Pearl Harbour.

2. It was a plot. Roosevelt and his government wanted to get the USA into the war but public opinion was against this. The government knew that Japan was ready to strike but gave no urgent warnings. They knew an attack would unite the nation in favour of war.

Source E

Roosevelt's plan was to defeat the Axis (Germany, Italy and Japan) by the maximum use of American industrial power but with the minimum possible expenditure of American lives.

J. L. Gaddis, 'The United States and the Origins of the Cold War', 1972

Source G   Production of arms 1940-43

	1940	1941	1943
Britain	3.5	6.5	11.1
Soviet Union	5.0	8.5	13.9
USA	1.5	4.5	37.5
TOTAL	**10.0**	**19.5**	**62.5**
Germany	6.0	6.0	13.8
Japan	1.0	2.0	4.5
Italy	0.75	1.0	–
TOTAL	**7.75**	**9.0**	**18.3**

(All figures in billions of dollars. Figures for Italy in 1943 are not available)

P. Kennedy, 'The Rise and Fall of the Great Powers', 1988

Source F   American fire power

An American warship uses its long range guns to blast positions held by Japanese troops on the island of Guam.

Source H

The first evidence of what the French are feeling today came from a woman living in a village. 'God has sent the British and the Americans', she said in a trembling voice. 'The Germans are afraid, I tell you, afraid.' As they came through the village German soldiers told her, 'The Allies have so many men, so much material. The sea is filled with their ships.'

BBC broadcast after British and American troops landed in France, June 1944

Checklist

- In June 1941 Germany invaded the Soviet Union. Hitler failed to gain a quick victory and was finally driven back by the Soviet armies.
- In 1941 the USA provided military equipment to help the British war effort.
- The USA entered the war in December 1941 after the Japanese attacked Pearl Harbour. Britain, the USA and the Soviet Union formed an alliance which eventually led to victory.

Activities

1. What effect might the picture in Source A have had on Americans opposed to the USA's entry into the war?

2. Why was the pilot in Source B surprised?

3. Judging by the picture in Source C, what did the Americans think of the Japanese?

4. Which of the explanations in Source D seems most likely? Give reasons for your answer.

5. a) How do Sources F, G and H show that Roosevelt's plan in Source E was put into practice?
   b) What do these sources tell us about Roosevelt's leadership style?

6. 'American industrial power was vital to the Allies' eventual victory.' Use the information in Sources G and H to support this statement.

6 A WORLD WAR

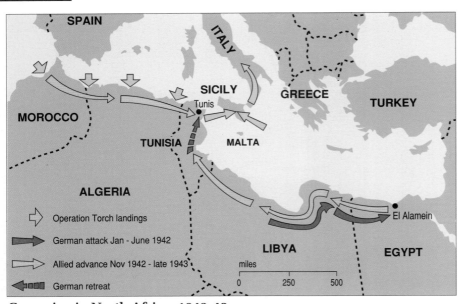

Campaign in North Africa, 1942-43

Operation Torch landings

German attack Jan - June 1942

Allied advance Nov 1942 - late 1943

German retreat

General Rommel (left), commander of the German Africa Corps with his staff officers

Themes

By the end of 1943 it seemed likely that, in time, the Allies were going to win the war. One indication of this was victory in North Africa (May 1943) followed by the invasion of Italy (July 1943). A second indication was the German surrender at Stalingrad (September 1943) followed by the start of the Soviet army's long march west. A third indication was the halting of the Japanese advance in Asia.

In 1944 Allied victory seemed even more likely. In June 1944 British and American troops landed in Normandy in northern France and began to push the German army back. The Germans were now under attack on two fronts.

This chapter looks at the worldwide scope of the war. It looks at the various military campaigns that led to the Allied victory in 1945. But the war was not just a military affair. Civilians were involved in the war to an extent that had never before been experienced. World War II was a 'total war'. This chapter also looks at the part played by civilians – under enemy occupation, under air attack, in the war effort and in resistance movements.

Tanks in the North Africa desert

Focus Activities

1. According to Rommel, why did the British win the battle of El Alamein?

2. The Americans and British poured military equipment and supplies into North Africa. This helped to turn the campaign in the Allies' favour. Why were equipment and supplies so important for desert warfare?

War in North Africa

European powers used their colonies as bases to carry the war into Africa. In 1940 the Italians launched an attack from Libya against the British in Egypt. They were driven back. In 1941 Germany sent forces under Rommel to North Africa. Rommel won several battles before being heavily defeated by the British Eighth Army (the 'Desert Rats') under General Montgomery at El Alamein in October 1942. In November 1942 Operation Torch began – British and American troops invaded Morocco and Algeria and advanced east to Tunis. With the British forces in Egypt advancing westwards, the Germans and Italians were caught in a pincer movement. In May 1943 Tunis was captured and the way opened for the Allies' invasion of Italy. The following extract gives Rommel's view of the German defeat at El Alamein.

British tanks breaking through the German minefield at El Alamein

I slept only a few hours and was back at my command vehicle again at 0500 hours. I learned that the British had spent the whole night attacking our front under cover of their artillery (long range guns) which in some places had fired as many as 500 rounds for every one of ours. I myself observed the attack that day from the north. Load after load of bombs cascaded down among my troops. I gave orders to the artillery to break up the British movement by concentrated fire, but we had too little ammunition to do it successfully. Late in the afternoon German and Italian dive bombers made an attempt to break up the British lorry columns moving northwest. Some 60 British fighters pounced on these slow machines and forced the Italians to jettison (dump) their bombs over their own lines. Never before in Africa had we seen such a density of anti-aircraft fire. Hundreds of British tracer shells criss-crossed the sky and the air became an absolute inferno of fire.

Finally a thrust by 160 British tanks succeeded in wiping out an already mauled battalion of the 164th Infantry Division. Violent fighting followed in which the remaining German and Italian tanks managed to force the enemy back. Tank casualties that day were 61 German and 56 Italian, all totally destroyed. Following their non-stop night attacks the RAF sent over formations of bombers at hourly intervals throughout the day. This not only caused considerable casualties but also began to produce serious signs of fatigue and a sense of inferiority among our troops.

The supply situation was now approaching disaster. A tanker which we had hoped would bring relief to the petrol situation had been bombed and sunk. There was only enough petrol left for another two or three days. What we should really have done now was to assemble all our motorised units and try to fling the British back in a planned counter attack. But we had not the petrol to do it.

E. Rommel, an account of the battle of El Alamein in October 1942 in 'The Rommel Papers', 1953

The scope of the war

Very little of the world's surface remained untouched by the war since it was fought by land, sea and air. People who had never left their own countries found themselves serving in the armed forces on different continents. Civilians were unable to escape the war. Great moments of heroism did not hide the enormous cruelty and suffering brought by global warfare fought with advanced technology.

Source A   The war in Europe and North Africa 1942-45

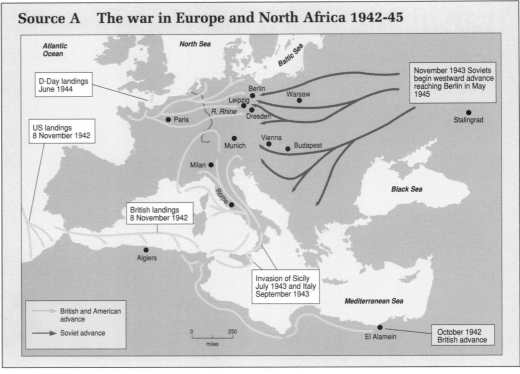

- D-Day landings June 1944
- US landings 8 November 1942
- British landings 8 November 1942
- Invasion of Sicily July 1943 and Italy September 1943
- November 1943 Soviets begin westward advance reaching Berlin in May 1945
- October 1942 British advance

Atlantic Ocean · North Sea · Baltic Sea · Black Sea · Mediterranean Sea

Berlin · Warsaw · Leipzig · Dresden · R. Rhine · Paris · Stalingrad · Vienna · Munich · Budapest · Milan · Rome · Algiers · El Alamein

Legend:
→ British and American advance
→ Soviet advance

0 — 250 miles

Source B   The Atlantic war

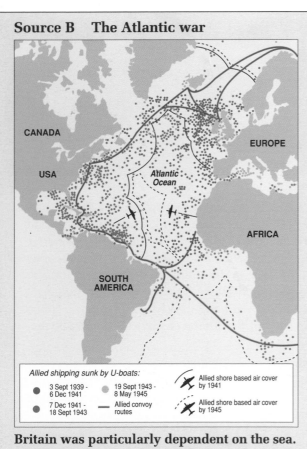

CANADA · USA · SOUTH AMERICA · EUROPE · AFRICA · Atlantic Ocean

Allied shipping sunk by U-boats:
- ● 3 Sept 1939 - 6 Dec 1941
- ● 7 Dec 1941 - 18 Sept 1943
- ● 19 Sept 1943 - 8 May 1945
- ✈ Allied shore based air cover by 1941
- ✈ Allied shore based air cover by 1945
- — Allied convoy routes

Britain was particularly dependent on the sea. Convoys (groups of ships under armed escort) kept open lines of supply, allowed the movement of troops and equipment and helped to prevent invasion.

Source C   The costs of war – shipping and bombs

The war at sea 1939 - 45

	1939	1940	1941	1942	1943	1944	1945
U - boat * losses (Germany)	9	22	35	85	287	241	153
Shipping losses (USA Britain) in tons	810,000	4,407,000	4,398,000	8,245,000	3,611,000	1,422,000	458,000
New constru-ction (USA) in registered tons	101,000	439,000	1,169,000	5,339,000	12,384,000	11,639,000	3,551,000
New constru-ction (Britain) in registered tons	231,000	780,000	815,,000	1,843,000	2,201,000	1,710,000	283,000
Total new construction in registered tons	332,000	1,219,000	1,984,000	7,182,000	14,585,000	13,349,000	3,834,000

* U - boats are German submarines.

Air bombardment 1940 - 45

	1940	1941	1942	1943	1944	1945
Bombs (in tons) Dropped on Germany	10,000	30,000	40,000	120,000	650,000	500,000
Dropped on Britain	36,844	21,858	3,260	2,298	9,151	761

Based on 'The Penguin Atlas of World History Volume 2', 1978

Source D The war in the Pacific 1941-45

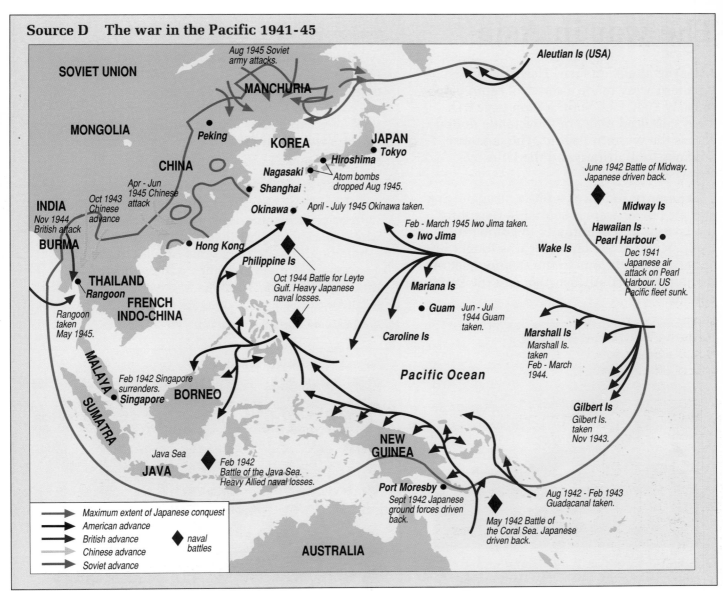

Aug 1945 Soviet army attacks.

SOVIET UNION

MANCHURIA

Aleutian Is (USA)

MONGOLIA

Peking

KOREA

JAPAN
Tokyo

CHINA

Hiroshima

Nagasaki

Atom bombs dropped Aug 1945.

Shanghai

June 1942 Battle of Midway. Japanese driven back.

Midway Is

Apr - Jun 1945 Chinese attack

Oct 1943 Chinese advance

Okinawa

April - July 1945 Okinawa taken.

Feb - March 1945 Iwo Jima taken.

Iwo Jima

Hawaiian Is

Pearl Harbour

Wake Is

Dec 1941 Japanese air attack on Pearl Harbour. US Pacific fleet sunk.

INDIA

Nov 1944 British attack

BURMA

Hong Kong

Philippine Is

Oct 1944 Battle for Leyte Gulf. Heavy Japanese naval losses.

Mariana Is

THAILAND

Rangoon

FRENCH INDO-CHINA

Guam

Jun - Jul 1944 Guam taken.

Caroline Is

Marshall Is

Marshall Is. taken Feb - March 1944.

Rangoon taken May 1945.

Pacific Ocean

MALAYA

Feb 1942 Singapore surrenders.

Singapore

BORNEO

Gilbert Is

Gilbert Is. taken Nov 1943.

SUMATRA

Java Sea

JAVA

Feb 1942 Battle of the Java Sea. Heavy Allied naval losses.

NEW GUINEA

Port Moresby

Sept 1942 Japanese ground forces driven back.

May 1942 Battle of the Coral Sea. Japanese driven back.

Aug 1942 - Feb 1943 Guadacanal taken.

AUSTRALIA

Legend:
- → Maximum extent of Japanese conquest
- → American advance
- → British advance
- → Chinese advance
- → Soviet advance
- ◆ naval battles

Source E The costs of war – death

Total deaths (estimates)

World War I	7 – 12 million
World War II	30 – 55 million

It is estimated that of the total number killed in World War II about two thirds were civilians. However estimates vary widely. Deaths resulting from World War II from five sources vary between 13.5 and 20.6 million for the Soviet Union, 4.2 and 7.8 million for Germany, 388,000 and 450,000 for Britain and 290,000 and 406,000 for the USA.

Activities

1. Using Sources A and D describe the areas controlled by the Allies in (a) October 1942 and (b) May 1945. What does this tell us about the changing fortunes of the Allies?

2. What do Sources B and C tell us about the course of the war in the Atlantic? Why do you think control of the Atlantic was important?

3. Use the evidence on these pages to explain:
   a) how the Allies managed to gain victory in 1945
   b) why the war is called a 'world war'.

4. Compare the sources on these pages with those on pages 4-5. What evidence is there that World War II was greater in scope and more destructive than World War I?

The war in Asia

After the attack on Pearl Harbour, the Japanese army made a series of rapid gains in early 1942 (see Source D on page 61). They captured many of the islands dotted across the western Pacific. The Japanese advance took Britain and the USA by surprise.

The war in Asia was a bitter struggle. Sea and air power were essential to recapture the islands and eventually to bombard Japan itself. Much of the land war was fought in appalling conditions in the steamy heat of the jungles of southeast Asia and the Pacific islands.

Source A

All through the Pacific and the Far East in 1941 I heard about the worthlessness of 'those little monkeys' (the Japanese). Everywhere I heard what we would do to them when the day of the great pushover came. One cruiser and a couple of aircraft carriers would destroy Tokyo.

Ernest Hemingway, 'Men at War', 1942

The Japanese not only out-fought us in Malaya, they out-thought us too. Dress and equipment were as light as possible and their speed at crossing country was remarkable. They had light weapons ideal for jungle fighting – tommy guns or light automatic weapons and hand grenades which were often lobbed from trees. They made great use of bicycles to move quickly.

I. Morrison, 'Malayan Postcript', 1942

Source B   Island hopping

Japanese forces on Wake Island under attack by the US, 1943. The Pacific war was slowly won by the American tactic of 'island hopping' – capturing one island and moving on to the next.

Source C   Jungle warfare

US marines in the jungle

Source D   Air and sea power

Part of the deck of the aircraft carrier 'Cowpens'. Naval and air strength were the key to victory in the Pacific.

Source E   Landing on the beach

I broke into a cold sweat. My stomach was tied in a knot, my knees nearly buckled. 'Hit the beach', yelled an officer. Men piled over the sides. At that instant a burst of machine gun fire snapped through the air. I caught a fleeting glimpse of a group of marines. Some fell as the bullets splashed among them and their buddies tried to help them as they struggled in knee deep water.

E. B. Sledge, a US marine, 'With the Old Breed at Peleliu and Okinawa', 1981

Source F Kamikaze planes

Kamikaze (suicide) planes were piloted by volunteers who flew their planes to crash and explode on the decks of Allied ships. They caused considerable damage – in one battle 24 ships were sunk by kamikaze planes on the same day. This picture shows a burning kamikaze plane on the deck of the US aircraft carrier, 'Saratoga', off Iwo Jima, 21 February 1945.

Source G Bombing Japan

Tokyo after an Allied bombing raid. As the Japanese retreated, the Allies came within range of mainland Japan. In March 1945 over 330 B29 bombers destroyed Tokyo, the capital of Japan, in a devastating fire bomb raid. Nearly 100,000 people died, 125,000 were injured and over 100,000 were made homeless.

Source H Prisoners of war

Surrender was seen as dishonourable by the Japanese and so prisoners were often treated very harshly. The guards could be kind but sometimes they beat us. They had complete power over people who could not strike back. Rules increased. Food decreased. Our ration was one cupful of thin rice gruel, five tablespoons of cooked rice, sometimes a few greens, a little sugar, sometimes a little salt and tea. I had meals of banana skins stolen from Japanese dustbins.

A. N. Keith, account of a camp in Borneo, 'Three Came Home', 1955

Out of 300,000 prisoners captured by the Japanese in the first months of the war, 100,000 were dead by the end of the war. The 200,000 survivors staggered emaciated (reduced to skin and bone) and exhausted from the scattered prison camps. Many felt a complete isolation – there was a wall of silence which their Japanese guards deliberately put around them. Letters took a year to reach the prisons and then were often left unopened by the Japanese for some time.

Marcel Junod, 'Red Cross: Warriors Without Weapons', 1951

Activities

1. 'The Allies underestimated the Japanese.' Explain this statement using Source A.

2. Using Sources B, C and D explain how the war in Asia differed from the war in Europe.

3. Using the map in Source D on page 61 and Sources B, E and G on these pages, explain the importance of air and sea power to war in the Pacific.

4. Look at Source F. The first Kamikaze attack was on 13 October 1944. What does the use of this tactic suggest about Japan's view of how the war was going?

5. Using Source H describe how the Japanese treated prisoners. Why do you think prisoners were treated this way?

Women at war

Women had played an important part in World War I. They played an even bigger part in World War II. In a world still dominated by men, women in World War II made a clear statement of their equal worth. Their role varied from country to country but they made a vital contribution in a time of total war.

Source A   British women

Working in the 'land army'

Making shells

Women between the ages of 18 and 50 were conscripted into war work unless they had husbands at home or young children. In Britain and the USA women were encouraged to join female branches of the armed forces. In neither country were women given fighting roles.

Source B

In Britain, the Soviet Union and the USA strong propaganda campaigns were launched to encourage women to join the war effort. This American picture shows 'Rosie the Riveter' holding a rivet gun with one foot on 'Mein Kampf' by Adolf Hitler.

Source C   Women in Germany

Poster for the women's section of the Hitler Youth. Goebbels (Minister for Propaganda) gave the view of the Nazi Party when he said, 'A woman's proper place is in the home'. There were no female branches of the German armed forces but women were expected to do volunteer work to help the armies at the front.

Source D   Women in the Soviet Union

Soviet pilots after a successful air battle in 1941.

Soviet women did play a fighting role as well as having a range of jobs behind the front line. In 1944 247,000 women belonging to the Young Communist League fought at the front. 88 women were awarded the highest Soviet medal, 'Hero of the Soviet Union'. These women included pilots, scouts, machine gunners, tank crews, nurses and radio operators.

J. Ericson, 'History Today', July 1990

Source E   Intelligence agents

Equipment used in France by Yvonne Cormeau. She was a French woman who lived in England. In 1943 she was parachuted into France. From then until the end of the war, with some very narrow escapes, she worked with the resistance (people who resisted the Nazi occupation of France), sending radio messages back to Britain. Many women played a courageous part in the gathering of information and in work with resistance groups (see pages 66-67).

Source F   After the war

Britain Women did types of work in the war which they had not done before and they continued this work after the war. Women also became more accustomed to working after marriage, another change which stuck. It was discovered, to the surprise of some men, that in most jobs a woman was the equal of a man – except when she came to be paid. ✗

P. Calvocoressi and G. Wint, 'Total War', 1972

USA Many women reported a new found sense of pride and independence when they realised they could handle traditional male jobs as well as or better than men. Others became accustomed to the additional income. Still others longed to return home. In most cases the choice was not theirs to make. Women were among the first to be fired after the war ended.

R. J. Maddox, 'The US and World War II', 1992

Soviet Union Postwar life for the front line women proved to be harsh. The liberated areas (areas freed from German occupation) were devastated, houses burned, schools ruined, orphans in need of care. Many returned prematurely aged and grey haired. Some never spoke of their days at war.

J. Ericson, 'History Today', July 1990

Activities

1. Look at Sources A to E.

   a) Describe women's contribution to the war effort. Can you think of other areas where they would have been important?

   b) What differences were there in the contributions made by women in Britain, the USA, Germany and the Soviet Union?

2. Suppose you were a woman in wartime. How would you help the war effort?

3. Look at Source F. How did women's wartime experience affect their lives after the war?

Resistance

People in countries occupied by an enemy had a difficult choice. They could resist, which was highly dangerous. They could collaborate (cooperate) with the occupiers. Or they could simply try to continue their normal lives as far as that was possible. In all the occupied countries a minority of people resisted occupation. Resistance groups used a variety of tactics and met with varying degrees of success.

Source B   French resistance

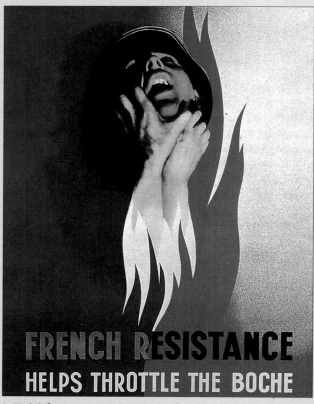

FRENCH RESISTANCE
HELPS THROTTLE THE BOCHE

A British poster supporting the French resistance movement. Boche means the Germans.

For supplies we relied on Paincheau. We needed petrol. The Germans kept it in tanks in a guarded building. One night Paincheau's men parked a tanker beside one wall of the building that was not guarded. One man, a stonemason, silently cut a hole in the wall. His comrades ran a pipe through to the tank and all night pumped out petrol. The mason then rebuilt the wall. They did the same the next night. Finally, before the Germans noticed the levels going down, Paincheau's men entered the building and put 200 kilos of sugar in the tanks.

G. Millar, 'Maquis', 1945

Source A   Aims of resistance groups

1. Intelligence – passing on information about the enemy.

2. Rescuing prisoners of war or preventing their capture.

3. Subversion – using all sorts of methods to damage the enemy such as sabotage (for example, blowing up railway lines), attacks on enemy troops or 'passive resistance' (refusing to obey orders).

Source C   Partisan armies

Soviet partisans prepare to blow up railway tracks. Partisans were armed civilians who fought the occupying troops. Large partisan armies operated in the Nazi occupied parts of the Soviet Union.

In Yugoslavia General Tito's army of 250,000 was the only resistance force to liberate an occupied country from within. Tito (in white) was a Croatian and a Communist. In 1945 he headed the Yugoslav government and held the country together for over 30 years.

Source D   Retaliation

Soviet partisans hanged for attacking German troops.

Source G   German resistance

Hitler shows Mussolini the result of the bomb that nearly killed him on 20 July 1944. By chance, Mussolini visited Hitler's headquarters that day.

The most difficult and dangerous resistance of all was probably that in Germany. In 1944 it nearly succeeded in removing Hitler. The bomb plot was planned by Lieutenant Colonel Count von Stauffenberg. He placed a briefcase containing a bomb under the table at a conference attended by Hitler. It was accidentally pushed further under the table so that when it exploded Hitler was saved by the table. Thousands were arrested and hundreds, including von Stauffenberg, were executed.

Source E   Sabotage and passive resistance in Norway

One party of nine men attacked the Norsk hydro heavy water plant at Verork, 80 miles west of Oslo. With a few plastic bombs they destroyed Germany's heavy water supplies and put paid to the Nazi's attempts to produce an atom bomb.

Quisling (a Norwegian collaborator who was put in charge of Norway by the Nazis) tried to revise the school history syllabus in line with Nazi ideas. Every history teacher in Norway refused to teach this. They were all arrested.

M. R. D. Foot, 'Resistance', 1976

Source F   Verdict on the resistance movement

In general resistance's strength in battlefield terms, in an age of armour and air warfare, was puny. But it had gigantic strength in moral terms. It gave back to people in the occupied countries the self-respect they had lost in the moment of occupation.

M. R. D. Foot, 'Resistance', 1976

Activities

1. Look at the sources on these pages.
   a) Why do you think only a minority of people joined resistance movements in the occupied countries?
   b) What examples of (i) active and (ii) passive resistance are mentioned?
   c) Can you think of any other ways of resisting that might have been used?
2. What does Source F tell us about the importance of resistance? Judging from the other sources do you agree with its conclusion? Explain your answer.
3. Suppose you had been a member of any one of the resistance groups mentioned on these pages. Write a passage from your diary explaining what you did and why you did it.

Mass bombing

The horrors of air attack had been introduced to the world by the German raid on Guernica in Spain (see page 28). The effects became far worse as the size and power of bombers increased during the Second World War. Attempts early in the war to bomb only military targets were soon abandoned. In total war no distinction was made by either side between civilians and armed forces. Protests about mass bombing were made but they were largely ignored. Air force leaders believed that it provided a way to win wars without having to defeat the enemy's armed forces on the ground.

Source A   The aims of mass bombing

Attack industrial centres where you:

a) do military damage by striking at the centres of war production and

b) achieve the greatest effect on morale by striking at the most sensitive part of the German population – namely the working class.

  The fact that air attacks destroy civilian life and property is no reason for regarding bombing as wrong, provided reasonable care has been taken.

Air Marshal Trenchard speaking in the 1920s

Source B   The bombers

The Avro Lancaster widely used in bombing raids on Germany

The Avro Lancaster was the most successful four engined aircraft built during the Second World War – in terms of its 'payload' (quantity of bombs carried), its range (distance it could fly) and its capacity to take and survive damage.

A. Verrier, 'The Bomber Offensive', 1968

Source C   Bombing German cities

Increasingly Allied Bomber Command relied on massive bombing raids on cities. One of the most horrific features of these raids was the use of incendiary (fire) bombs. These could create firestorms – gusts of flame at 1000°C travelling at over 100 miles an hour.

  They were in a small field and the houses on one side were alight. A great flame was shooting straight towards them – a flame as high as the houses and nearly as wide as the whole street. As she stared in fascination, the giant flame jerked back and then shot forward towards them again. 'My God, what is it?' she said. 'It's a firestorm', the man replied. 'In a minute there'll be dozens of flames like that. We must run.'

E. Wendel describing the Allied raid on Hamburg in 'Hausfrau at War', 1957

Source D   Precision bombing

The Mohne Dam is holed. The 'dam busters' attack was made from a height of 20 metres by 19 Lancaster bombers. 8 aircraft were lost and 54 men killed. The dam was holed but there was no long term damage. Although aircraft navigation and bomb aiming improved during the war, it still remained difficult to bomb precisely. Even if targets were hit, the result was usually heavy losses of crew and planes.

Source E   Dresden 1945

On the night of 13 to 14 February 1945, 805 British planes dropped 2,600 tons of bombs on the centre of the German town of Dresden. Over 50,000 died in a horrific firestorm. Dresden had little military importance. Sir Arthur Harris, Head of Bomber Command, believed that 'terror' raids on German cities could win the war.

Source G

The change from the 'precision' bombing of military objectives to the present 'obliteration' bombing of whole areas with their churches, libraries, schools, hospitals, museums and vulnerable human beings came with the appointment of Sir Arthur Harris to the control of Bomber Command on 3 March 1942. This is a policy of murder and massacre in the name of the British people.

Vera Brittain, 'Testament of a Peace Lover', December 1943

Activities

1. According to Source A how was mass bombing a way to 'win wars without having to defeat the enemy's armed forces'?

2. Using the sources on these pages give the arguments for and against:
   a) precision bombing b) mass bombing.

3. You are a journalist in 1946. Using Sources C, E and F, write an article entitled, 'The bombing experience'. Include interviews with a British bomber pilot and a German civilian.

4. Look at Sources G and H. What do you think the Mayor of Dresden would have written to the organisers of the ceremony to honour 'Bomber' Harris?

Source F   RAF bombing raids

Source H   'Bomber Harris'

Statue of Sir Arthur 'Bomber' Harris, unveiled by the Queen Mother in May 1992. News that this statue was to be unveiled at an official ceremony produced strong protests from many Germans, especially the Mayor of Dresden. Until 1992 Harris was the only wartime commander not to receive an official statue.

War in Europe - the final stages

At Tehran in December 1943 Britain and the USA had promised the Soviet Union to start a second front by invading France. That promise was kept. On 6 June 1944, 'D-Day', the invasion known as 'Operation Overlord' was launched. The final phase in the struggle against the Axis had begun.

The Germans put up strong resistance and it was May 1945 before the war in Europe ended. With the steady advance of the Soviets from the east, Germany eventually collapsed in the face of its greatest strategic nightmare – war on two fronts (see Source A on page 60).

Source A   The Normandy beaches

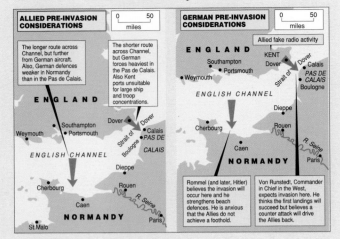

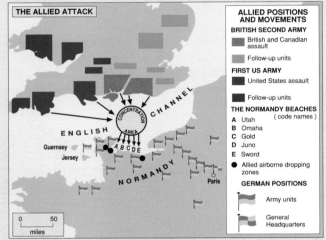

These maps indicate some of the reasons for the choice of Normandy for the invasion. The Germans did not know that Normandy had been chosen.
Maps based on P. Calvocoressi and G. Wint, 'Total War', 1972

Source B   German preparations

Rommel (the German Commander) believed that, 'The war would be won or lost on the beaches'. He tried to strengthen defences with minefields and with a variety of obstacles to wreck the landing craft. But problems remained.

By 1944 Hitler had seriously weakened the German military command system. Now the control of every small detail came from Hitler himself. He hated the General Staff who made decisions about military operations and split it. No Allied landing could ever have been defeated by us without an air force and this we utterly lacked.

General von Schweppenburg, 'Articles of War', 1964

Source C   The landings

A vast force was gathered in southern England along with huge quantities of equipment.
Troops: 2 million (1.5 million from the USA)
Boats: 5,000
Aircraft: 7,500

The landing craft came under fire. The enemy fortifications had not been knocked out. Men loaded with equipment and explosives were excellent targets as they unloaded. One boat grounded in water 2 to 3 metres deep and the men were enveloped in intense fire from automatic weapons. Troops dived under water, trying to save the wounded. Many of them died.

'Omaha Beachhead', American Forces in Action Series, 1945

The British Second Army landing at Normandy, 6 June 1944

Source D   Crossing the Rhine

The Allies cross the Rhine into Germany in March 1945. In some areas they outnumbered the Germans 10:1. But it was their equipment rather than numbers which finally overpowered the German army. Fighting continued throughout April but the Germans could do little to halt the Allies' advance.

Source E   Hitler's last days

Hitler, on his 56th birthday, congratulates Hitler Youth. They had been ordered to defend Berlin but many did not even know how to load and fire their guns. Ten days later, on 30 April 1945, Hitler shot himself in his underground bunker (shelter) in Berlin. His body was taken outside, doused with petrol and burned.

Source F   The fall of Berlin

A soldier raises the red flag over the Reichstag as the Soviet armies complete the capture of Berlin. On 8 May 1945 the war in Europe finally ended.

Checklist

- By 1943 the war was worldwide with fronts in Europe, Africa and Asia.
- Women played a vital role in the war effort.
- A minority of people actively resisted occupying forces.
- Mass bombing reduced many cities to rubble and killed many thousands of civilians.
- Germany's surrender in May 1945 ended the war in Europe.

Activities

1. Read Sources A to C.
   a) Why did the Allies choose the Normandy beaches rather than Calais to launch the invasion?
   b) What were the main strengths and the main problems facing (i) the Allies and (ii) the Germans at the time of the 1944 invasions?
2. What evidence do Sources D and F provide to suggest that the Germans were completely overpowered in the final stages of the war in Europe?
3. 'By April 1945 the Nazis were desperate.' Explain this statement using Source E.

7 THE HOLOCAUST

The site of Auschwitz concentration camp today. Auschwitz was a death camp. The words on the gate read, 'work brings freedom'.

Children freed from Auschwitz in 1945

Themes

The word holocaust means 'complete destruction'. When people use the word holocaust today they are usually thinking of a single episode in history – the slaughter of 6 million civilians, most of them Jews, who lived under Nazi rule. Throughout history there have been occasions when large numbers of people have been massacred. Often such massacres have occurred during wars. The Holocaust, however, is different. It was carefully planned by the Nazi government. A system was set up whose only purpose was to kill as many of its victims as quickly as possible. On no other occasion have government departments been set up with the sole purpose of organising mass murder. About six million civilians were killed in the Holocaust. If the war had continued there were plans to kill at least another five million.

This chapter looks at the following questions.

- What events led to the Holocaust?
- What happened during the Holocaust and why?
- Who was responsible for the Holocaust?

Focus Activities

1. There is no mention of the Nazis in Richard Dimbleby's report in the Focus but it tells us much about Nazi Germany. What does it tell us?

2. Describe the effect that Richard Dimbleby wanted to create. How do you know that he was trying to create this effect? Would you say that the Focus is a useful historical source?

3. What evidence is there in the Focus to suggest that the Holocaust was different from any other episode in World War II?

Inside Bergen-Belsen concentration camp

On 15 April 1945 the British army reached Bergen-Belsen near Hanover in northwest Germany. Here they found a concentration camp (prison camp). Belsen was not one of the death camps set up by the Nazis. These were mainly found to the east. Belsen had been set up as an ordinary prison camp. But as the German army retreated in 1944, prisoners from other concentration camps were sent to Belsen to prevent them falling into the hands of the Allies. The facilities at Belsen were unable to cope with these extra prisoners and by April 1945 there were 40,000 prisoners living in appalling conditions. Below, a BBC reporter, Richard Dimbleby, reports on what he found.

There were so many unburied bodies at Belsen that a bulldozer had to be used. The bodies had to be removed as quickly as possible to prevent the spread of disease.

I picked my way over corpse after corpse until I heard one voice raised above the gentle moaning. I found a girl. She was a living skeleton, impossible to tell her age since she had practically no hair left and her face was a yellow parchment sheet with two holes in it for eyes. She was stretching out her stick of an arm and gasping, 'English, English, medicine, medicine'. She was trying to cry but hadn't enough strength. Beyond her down the passage and in the hut there were the convulsive movements of dying people too weak to raise themselves from the floor.

In the shade of the tree lay a great collection of bodies. I walked about trying to count. There were perhaps 150 flung down on each other, all naked, all so thin their yellow skin glistened like stretched rubber on their bones. At one end of the pile a group of men and women had gathered around a fire. They were using rags and old shoes taken from the bodies to keep it alight and they were heating soup. Close by was the enclosure where 500 children between the ages of 5 and 12 had been kept. They were not as hungry as the rest because the women had sacrificed themselves to keep the children alive. Babies were born at Belsen, some of them shrunken little things that could not live because their mothers could not feed them.

There was no privacy of any kind. Women stood naked at the side of the truck washing in cupfuls of water taken from British Army trucks. Others searched themselves for lice and examined each other's hair. Sufferers from dysentery leaned against the huts straining helplessly. All around them was this awful tide of exhausted people. Just a few held out their withered hands to us as we passed. I have never seen British soldiers so moved to cold fury as the men who opened the Belsen camp this week and who are now trying to save the prisoners who are not too far gone in starvation.

Richard Dimbleby, BBC radio broadcast, 19 April 1945

The Nazis and racism

The Nazis were racists. They believed that some 'races' were better than others. Today people usually think of race in terms of skin colour – for example, a racist today might claim that a white person is better than a black person. Nazis believed this but they went further. According to the Nazis, the 'Aryan' race was the 'master race'. The ideal Aryan was a white person with blond hair and blue eyes. But membership of the Aryan race did not just depend on appearance. It also depended on a person's beliefs and behaviour. For example, the Nazis believed that all Jews belonged to an 'inferior race' – as did gypsies, Communists and homosexuals.

After the First World War many Germans felt frustrated and resentful. They had lost the war and felt they had lost the peace. The German economy had collapsed and there was widespread poverty and unemployment (see pages 22-23). In situations like this people often look for a scapegoat – someone to blame. Hitler was in no doubt who was to blame for Germany's downfall. In the 1920s he repeated the same message time and again, 'It is the Jew who is ruining our country'.

Racism is a type of hatred. Hatred can easily lead to violence. When the Nazis gained power in 1933 their racist beliefs were well known but few people expected them to use violence against the people they ruled. Before the Second World War broke out, however, the first steps towards the Holocaust had been taken.

Source A

If I am ever really in power the destruction of the Jews will be my first and most important job. As soon as I have the power I shall have gallows after gallows erected. Then Jews will be hanged one after another and will stay hanging until they stink.

Letter from Hitler to Josef Hell, 1922

Source B   Nazi propaganda

This poster says, 'We peasants are clearing out the muck'. It shows an Aryan German peasant shovelling away Communists and Jews.

Source C   Boycott of the Jews, April 1933

Hitler became Chancellor on 30 January 1933. Two months later the Nazis made their first attempt to put their racist ideas into practice. They organised a boycott of the Jews. This picture shows a Nazi guard outside a Jewish shop.

Overnight, Jews in Germany have become second class citizens. Yesterday the Nazis proposed an absolute boycott of the Jews. At 10 am on 1 April all Jewish businesses will be occupied by the Nazis and forced to close. Jewish lawyers will be denied access to the courts. Department stores will be occupied. No Nazi will be allowed to associate with a Jew. The mood here is at rock bottom. No one knows how it will all end. Bloodshed, perhaps.

Diary of an unknown Jewish banker, 30 March 1933

Source D   The Nuremberg Laws 1935

1. Only a person of German or similar blood is a citizen of the Reich (Germany). A Jew is not a citizen of the Reich. He has no vote. He may not hold public office.

2. Marriage between Jews and citizens of German blood is forbidden.

3. Sexual relations outside marriage between Jews and German citizens are forbidden.

4. Jews are forbidden to display the national flag or the national colours.

'Law for the Protection of German Blood and German Honour', September 1935

Source F   Kristallnacht (Crystal night)

At the beginning of November 1938 a Jewish youth murdered a German diplomat in Paris. This was the excuse Nazi leaders had been waiting for. On 9-10 November Nazis attacked Jews throughout Germany. 91 Jews were killed and 30,000 sent to concentration camps. Jewish businesses and synagogues (places of worship) were destroyed. This was called 'Crystal night' because of all the broken glass. Immediately afterwards it was made illegal for Jews to attend German schools and universities and they were banned from cinemas, theatres and swimming pools.

The brutal measures against the Jews have caused great indignation among the population. People spoke their minds quite openly and many Aryans were arrested as a result. When it became known that a Jewish woman had been taken from her bed during childbirth even a police official said that it was too much. As a result, he was arrested too. After the Jews who are going to be the next victims? That is what people are asking.

We should not overlook the fact that there are people who do not defend the Jews. When the Jewish synagogue was burning in Berlin a large number of women could be heard saying, 'That's the right way to do it – it's a pity there aren't any Jews inside, that would be the best way to smoke out the whole lousy lot of them'.

'The Reports on Germany', SOPADE (Socialist Democrats in Exile), November 1938

Source E   The Berlin Olympics 1936

Jesse Owens at the 1936 Olympic Games in Berlin. The Nazis used the games as an opportunity to put the Third Reich on show. But when Jesse Owens, a black American athlete, won 4 gold medals, Hitler refused to congratulate him.

Activities

1. What does Source A tell us about Hitler's beliefs? Why is the date of this letter important?

2. Using Sources C, D and F describe how the lives of German Jews were affected by measures taken by the Nazis in the 1930s. What evidence is there that they became second class citizens?

3. a) 'Jews were not the only target of Nazi racism in the 1930s.' Explain this statement using Sources B and E.

   b) What evidence is there on these pages to suggest that Jews were the main target?

4. Look at Source F. How did ordinary German people react to Nazi policy towards Jews? Why do you think they reacted in these ways?

The final solution

The Nazis aimed to make Germany a 'racially pure' country. Before the war this meant persuading non-Aryans to go and live elsewhere. By 1939 nearly half of the 525,000 people officially defined as non-Aryans by the Nazis had emigrated from Germany.

1941 was a turning point. By then the Nazis had conquered much of Europe and many people living in the newly conquered areas were non-Aryans. For example, over 3 million Jews lived in Poland before it was attacked in 1939. As soon as Poland had been invaded, the Nazis began to round up Jews and force them to live in areas sealed off from the outside world. These areas became known as 'ghettos'.

In June 1941 Hitler gave the order to attack the Soviet Union. As the German army advanced into the Soviet Union, leaders of the SS (Secret Police) organised an 'experiment'. Special groups of SS officers were ordered to follow the army and kill all Jews and any other 'racially impure' people they could find. By January 1942 1.4 million civilians had been shot.

The experiment was judged a 'success'. On 23 October 1941 Himmler, the Head of the SS, issued new orders which became known as the 'final solution'. No longer were non-Aryans allowed to emigrate from areas under Nazi control. They were sent east to death camps. Special gas chambers were built in these camps – the Nazis found gassing to be a more efficient way of killing large numbers of people than shooting. On 8 December 1941 the first victims were gassed to death. The Holocaust had begun.

Source A   The death camps

The 'selection' at Auschwitz, one of the death camps set up by the Nazis. A group of Hungarian Jews has just arrived by train. SS officers are separating those to be gassed from those to be used as slave labour in the IG Farben chemical factory attached to the camp. In 1944 12,000 people were killed in the gas chambers every day. The gas chambers were built to look like shower rooms so that the victims did not know what to expect. The chemical used in the gas chambers, 'Cyclon B', was one of the products manufactured in the IG Farben factory.

Source B   A survivor of Auschwitz

In June 1943 we were deported from Berlin. After two days and nights in a train we reached Auschwitz. The stench and the hysterical screaming were terrible. When we arrived we were forced out by guards shouting. Our luggage was left behind and we never saw it again. Next a checkpoint where SS officers asked our age and occupation. I made myself two years older than I was and said I was a mechanic.

Out of about 300 men and 60 women, around 100 were admitted to the camp. The rest were given 'special treatment'. In other words, they were gassed. When married couples with children arrived, the man automatically went along to be gassed with his family. At Auschwitz numbers were tattooed onto your arms. There were no more names.

A typical day in a concentration camp: getting up amid noises and shouting – everything on the run. Then out onto the main square for roll call. If someone had dropped dead he was dragged out to even up the count. As it was getting light we marched off to work accompanied by the music of the prisoners' band. If someone was hanged the band played afterwards by order of the SS.

The IG Farben factory covered about 3 square miles. You worked like a dog until you collapsed. I had to be dragged to work often enough because I literally couldn't stand up any more. If I survived the 1½ years it was only because time and again I met someone who helped me.

Hans Radziewski, a Jew who survived Auschwitz, interviewed in 1989-90

Source C

In the course of the final solution the Jews should be brought to the east. Separated by sex, the Jews capable of work will join labour gangs. Doubtless a large part will fall away through natural reduction. The remainder will have to be dealt with appropriately. In the course of the final solution Europe will be combed from west to east. For the moment evacuated Jews will be brought to ghettos from where they will be transported farther to the east.

R. Heydrich (Deputy Head of the SS), Wannsee Conference Minutes, January 1942

Source E   The number of people killed

Although the SS recorded the number of people killed in camps, some records have been lost and they do not include people killed elsewhere. The figures below are based on the Jewish population before and after the war. One leading Nazi, Eichmann, said at his trial in 1961 that he knew that at least 6 million Jews had been killed.

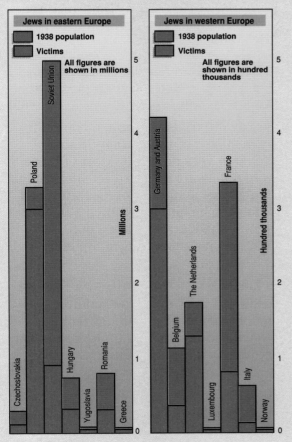

Source D   Disposing of bodies at Dachau

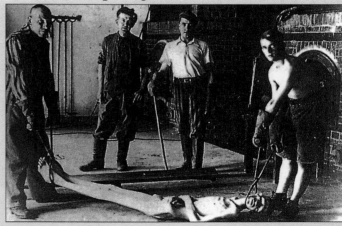

Disposing of so many corpses was a problem that the Nazis never solved. At Dachau inmates were forced to incinerate corpses in tiny furnaces. This photograph was taken by a Nazi guard.

Source F

Re: the utilisation of cut hair. In response to a report, the Chief of the SS Main Office, SS officer Pohl, has ordered that all human hair cut off in concentration camps should be utilised. Human hair will be processed for industrial felt and spun into thread. Female hair which has been cut and combed out will be used as thread to make socks for U-boat (submarine) crews and felt stockings for railway workers. You are instructed, therefore, to store the hair of female prisoners after it has been disinfected. Cut hair from male prisoners can only be used if it is at least 20 mm in length. The amounts of human hair collected each month, separated into female and male hair, must be reported on the fifth of each month to this office.

SS Officer R. Glucks, Circular, 6 August 1942

Activities

1. Using Sources A and B explain how the Nazis attempted to bring about the 'final solution of the Jewish question'.
2. What do Sources C, D and F tell us about the attitude of Nazis involved in the organisation of the final solution?
3. Although the figures in Source E are not exact they provide useful historical information. Is this true? Explain your answer.

Understanding the Holocaust

Once the decision to go ahead with the final solution had been taken, thousands of people became directly involved. SS officers were needed to round up the non-Aryans, trains had to be arranged and driven, the camps had to be guarded. But despite the number of people involved, attempts were made to keep the whole process secret.

It was only after the Allies had won the war that the extent of the Holocaust became clear. Since then many people have been trying to understand how it could have been allowed to happen. An important question to answer is, 'Who was responsible?' Some people have argued that Hitler was personally to blame. Others say that it was the Nazi system rather than Hitler himself. A third group argues that the German population as a whole was in some way responsible. At the end of the war this question was particularly important because the Allies had to decide what measures should be taken to make sure there was a lasting peace.

Source A   The Nuremberg trials

Goering in the dock at Nuremberg

At the end of the war Hitler, Goebbels (Minister for Propaganda) and Himmler (Head of the SS) committed suicide. All three had played an important part in making the decision to go ahead with the final solution.

After the war, 22 leading Nazis were put on trial at Nuremberg. The most senior was Hitler's deputy, Goering. In July 1941 he had signed an order instructing the SS, 'to make all necessary preparations to bring about a total solution of the Jewish problem'. Goering was sentenced to hang but committed suicide beforehand. The other defendants were hanged or given long prison sentences.

Over the next 20 years 20,000 people were convicted by either Allied or German courts for crimes committed in Nazi Germany. Most were convicted for their part in the Holocaust.

Source B

The Waffen-SS had nothing to do with the concentration camps. We were soldiers. The Waffen-SS was separate from the 'Death's Head' battalions which were the guard battalions for the concentration camps. Inside there was a small camp command consisting of maybe 12 men. That was all the SS actually had in the camps. Today people say that we were all Nazis. But we considered ourselves to be soldiers. We wanted nothing to do with what happened in the concentration camps, for God's sake! I would never have supported anything like that.

Otto Kumm, an SS Commander during the war, interviewed in 1989-90

Source C

I was an expert witness at 150 trials in German courts. It is generally argued by members of the Waffen-SS that they have a clean slate. I am very doubtful. Most of those accused of murder were not aware of the seriousness of their crimes. For instance, one man did not feel burdened in the least because, after all, he had only killed 5,000. He said, 'Why am I being punished? It was only 5,000. Ohlendorf killed 20,000 – that's something completely different.'

Some people even claim that the things that are said to have happened at Auschwitz are lies. This is complete nonsense. I know the documents. There are SS reports revealing how many Jews had been killed up to a certain point in time and that was already 3 million. I'm talking about official SS statistics. Everything was precisely recorded.

Hans Gunther Seraphin, a commander of Soviet volunteers in the German army during the war, interviewed in 1989-90

Source D

One day our neighbour in Berlin who worked at SS Headquarters told my father, 'Mr Herz, we've never spoken but I'd like to tell you that it would be better if you disappeared for a few weeks'. We took my father to a small country village. He spent the first week shut up in a tiny room in my great-aunt's house. A Nazi member lived nearby. One day he came to my great-aunt and said, 'You can't fool me. Hanns is here. I heard him cough and I know that cough. Why should he hide? He can come out, nothing's going to happen to him here.' My father came out and they talked. Then the Nazi brought two other Nazis and they played cards every night. Whenever a bigwig from the Party visited, they warned him.

H. P. Herz, a half-Jew who survived the war, interviewed in 1989-90

Source E   Denazification

One of the Allies' first acts after taking control of Germany was to make a film showing the appalling conditions they had found in the concentration camps. This film was sent to cinemas throughout Germany and every German citizen was forced to watch it. Historians R. Manvell and H. Fraenkel noted, 'Public reaction to the newsreel naturally varied. Many saw the film in silence. Some women wept. Others laughed hysterically and then burst into tears. Men were seen with bowed heads.' After the screening shown in this photograph two girls were made to see the film again on their own because they had been seen laughing on their way out.

Activities

1. Look at Sources A, B and C. Many of the SS officers on trial after the war argued they were not responsible for the Holocaust because they were only obeying orders. Would you agree that this is a reasonable defence? Explain your answer.

2. Using Sources C and D give the arguments for and against the view that all Nazis were in some way to blame for the Holocaust.

3. Look at Source E.
   a) Why do you think German citizens were forced to watch the film?
   b) Suppose you had been in the audience. Write down what you saw and how you felt about it.

4. What does the information in this chapter tell us about the sort of leader Hitler was?

Checklist

- The Nazis were racists. They believed they belonged to a 'master race' of Aryans. They encouraged people to hate non-Aryans, especially Jews.

- The Nazis said that they wanted to make Germany a 'racially pure' country. Before 1941 this meant persuading non-Aryans to emigrate. After 1941 they decided that all non-Aryans should be killed.

- By the end of the war at least 6 million non-Aryans had been killed. Most of the victims were Jews. Most of the killing took place in purpose built death camps.

- Opinions are divided about who should be held responsible for the Holocaust.

8 THE ATOM BOMB

The ruins of Hiroshima, August 1945

Themes

On 6 August 1945 a new kind of weapon, the atom bomb, was dropped on Hiroshima, Japan. The city was totally devastated. 80,000 people were killed immediately and another 40,000 were injured. Many more were to die later from their injuries and from radiation poisoning caused by exposure to radiation from the bomb.

On 9 August 1945 a second atom bomb was dropped on Nagasaki, a Japanese port. This time 40,000 people were killed. Japan surrendered and the war was over. But the invention of the atom bomb meant the beginning of a nuclear age.

This chapter looks at these questions.

- What is an atom bomb?
- Why did the Allies want to build an atom bomb?
- What made them decide to use it against Japan?
- What were the effects of the first atom bombs?
- How did nuclear technology develop after the war?

Focus Activities

1. Why does the newspaper say that the atom bomb has 'changed the world'?

2. Describe how the pilots who dropped the atom bomb reacted to what they had done. Why did they react in this way?

3. You are a survivor of the Hiroshima bombing. You have been through air raids before but this was something different. What do you write in your diary that night?

FOCUS

DAILY EXPRESS

No. 14,094 — Lighting-up: 9.39 pm to 4.33 am — TUESDAY AUGUST 7 1945 — Weather: Cool, showers — One Penny

Smoke hides city 16 hours after greatest secret weapon strikes

THE BOMB THAT HAS CHANGED THE WORLD

Japs told 'Now quit'

THE Allies disclosed last night that they have used against Japan the most fearful device of war yet produced—an atomic bomb.

It was dropped at 20 minutes past midnight, London time, yesterday on the Japanese port and army base of Hiroshima, 190 miles west of Kobe.

The city was blotted out by a cloud of dust and smoke. Sixteen hours later reconnaissance pilots were still waiting for the cloud to lift to let them see what had happened.

The bomb was a last warning. Now leaflets will tell the Japanese what to expect unless their Government surrenders.

So great will be the devastation if they do not surrender that Allied land forces may be able to invade without opposition.

20,000 tons in golf ball

ONE atomic bomb has a destructive force equal to that of 20,000 tons of T.N.T., or five 1,000-plane raids. This terrific power is packed in a space of little more than golf ball size.

Experts estimate that the bomb can destroy anything on the surface in an area of at least two square miles—twice the size of the City of London.

When it was tested after being assembled in a farmhouse in the remote desert of New Mexico, a steel tower used for the experiment vaporised; two men standing nearly six miles away were blown down; blast effect was felt 300 miles away.

And, at Albuquerque, 120 miles away, a blind girl cried "What is that?" when the flash lighted the sky before the explosion could be heard.

BLAST FELT 300 MILES FROM BOMB TEST

Steel tower turned to vapour

From C. V. R. THOMPSON: New York, Monday

Suddenly a glaring pinkish light appeared in the sky, accompanied by an unnatural tremor which was followed almost immediately by a wave of heat and a wind which swept away everything in its path. Many were killed instantly, others lay writhing on the ground screaming in agony from the intolerable pain of their burns. Everything standing upright in the way of the blast – walls, houses, factories and other buildings – was completely destroyed.

Hiroshima survivor

What kind of bomb was it that had destroyed Hiroshima? Perhaps it was a new weapon! Whatever it was, it was beyond me. Damage of that order could have no explanation.

Dr Hachiya, 'Hiroshima Diary'

A bright light filled the plane. The first shock wave hit us. We were eleven and a half miles from the atomic explosion but the whole plane cracked and crinkled from the blast. We turned back to look at Hiroshima. The city was hidden by that awful cloud boiling up, mushrooming, terrible and incredibly tall. I remember Lewis pounding my shoulder, saying, 'Look at that! Look at that! Look at that!'

Paul Tibbets, pilot of the 'Enola Gay', the plane that dropped the bomb on Hiroshima

I thought, 'Thank God the war is over and I don't have to get shot at any more. I can go home.'

Van Kirk, in the plane with Tibbets

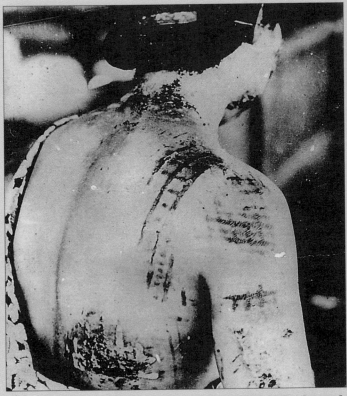

This woman has had the pattern of her kimono (robe) burned on to her skin by the atom bomb dropped on Hiroshima.

The race for the bomb

In 1938 a German scientist, Otto Hahn, discovered nuclear fission – the splitting of atoms. In certain materials, such as uranium, splitting the atom releases huge amounts of heat energy and radiation.

When the world heard about Hahn's findings, it did not take long for scientists to realise that nuclear energy and nuclear weapons would now be possible. Germany, Britain and the USA all began nuclear research programmes in the race to get the 'superbomb'.

Source B   Otto Hahn

I'm going to do it (research into the atom bomb) but if, by my work, Hitler gets the bomb I shall commit suicide.

Otto Hahn, 1939

Source D

If such a weapon is possible, there will be somebody who makes it, and if there is somebody who makes it, it will be used. Either we will overcome war, or we will destroy ourselves.

C. F. von Weizsacker, a scientist who worked on Germany's nuclear research programme, 'Hitler's Bomb', BBC TV, February 1992

Source A

An atom bomb exploding in a test in the Nevada desert, USA. Apart from their power, what makes nuclear weapons so different is 'radioactive fallout'. The explosion sucks huge amounts of earth into the air. Particles of earth become contaminated by radiation and fall back to the ground. People exposed to these particles can suffer radiation sickness which often leads to death.

Source C   Germany abandons nuclear research

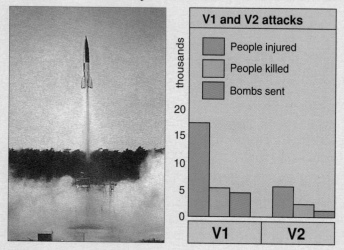

A V2 rocket

By February 1942 the German army had decided to abandon research into the atom bomb. At this point the German government expected the war to last only another year or two and was looking for quick results. It decided that all resources and efforts should be poured into rocket research. Although many V1 and V2 rockets landed in Britain (see Source C, page 46) their destructive power was minute compared to the atom bomb.

Source E   The Manhattan Project

Robert Oppenheimer (right) discussing the atom bomb

Frightened that the Nazis would develop an atom bomb first, the USA and Britain launched the Manhattan Project, a nuclear research programme, led by Robert Oppenheimer in Los Alamos, New Mexico in the USA.

Source F

It's what kept the Manhattan Project going, this fear of Nazi nuclear weapons raining down on Europe, or the United States. No one could argue with the idea that, if nuclear weapons are possible and if the Germans are working on them, then we have to get them first.

Dr Mark Walker, historian, 'Hitler's Bomb', BBC TV, February 1992

Source G

I have no hope of clearing my conscience. The things we are working on are so terrible that nothing will save our souls. But, if we have a slim chance of survival, it lies in the possibility to get rid of wars.

Edward Teller, physicist who worked on the Manhattan Project

Source H

An imaginary situation in which two atom bombs are exploded over New York.

Activities

1. Why was the atom bomb a greater threat than V1 and V2 rockets? Explain using Sources A, C and H.

2. a) Why were the scientists in Sources B, D and G so worried about the atom bomb?

   b) Why did they agree to work on the bomb?

3. Using Sources D, E, F and H explain why it was so important for the Allies to be the first to make the atom bomb.

4. Should scientists work on nuclear weapons? Give both sides of the argument.

Japan surrenders

In July 1945 American scientists carried out the first successful atom bomb test, two months after Germany had surrendered.

The war against Japan continued. The USA was winning but 6,812 soldiers were killed fighting for the island of Iwo Jima (February 1945) and 7,374 were killed fighting for the island of Okinawa (April to June 1945). On 12 April 1945 President Roosevelt died and Vice President Harry Truman took over. President Truman was worried that many more American troops would be killed before Japan surrendered.

At a meeting in Potsdam on the outskirts of Berlin (July to August 1945) the Allied leaders announced that, unless the Japanese surrendered, the atom bomb would be used. Japan refused to surrender and on 6 August 1945 an atom bomb was dropped on Hiroshima. Still the Japanese refused to surrender. Three days later an atom bomb was dropped on Nagasaki. On 14 August 1945 Japan finally surrendered.

Source A   Potsdam

Churchill (left), Truman (centre) and Stalin at Potsdam

We call upon the government of Japan to proclaim now the unconditional surrender of all the Japanese armed forces. The alternative for Japan is complete and utter destruction.

Joint ultimatum to Japan, Potsdam, July 1945

Source B   Japanese honour

A Japanese kamikaze pilot puts on his ceremonial scarf before a mission. Kamikaze planes were packed with explosives. The pilots faced almost certain death as they dived into Allied warships (see page 63). Capture or surrender was considered dishonourable.

The Japanese are the bravest people I have ever met. In attack they simply came on, using all their skill and rage, until they were stopped by death. In defence they held their ground with furious determination. They had to be killed company by company, squad by squad, man by man to the last.

J. Masters, 'The Road Past Mandalay', 1961

Source C

The Japanese began the war from the air at Pearl Harbour. They have been repaid many times over. And the end is not yet. We are now prepared to obliterate every productive enterprise the Japanese have above ground in any city. We shall destroy their docks, their factories and their communications. Let there be no mistake. We shall completely destroy Japan's power to make war.

President Truman's announcement that the bomb had been dropped on Hiroshima, 7 August 1945

Source D   Hiroshima

I WRITE THIS AS A WARNING TO THE WORLD

In Hiroshima, thirty days after the first atomic bomb destroyed the city and shook the world, people are still dying mysteriously and horribly from an unknown something which I can only describe as the atomic plague.

The police chief welcomed me eagerly as the first Allied reporter to reach the city. He took me to hospitals where victims of the bomb are being treated. There I found people who, when the bomb fell, suffered absolutely no injuries but now are dying from the strange after-effects. For no apparent reason their health began to fail. They lost appetite. Their hair fell out. Bluish spots appeared on their bodies. And then bleeding began from ears, nose and mouth. At first, the doctors told me, they thought these were symptoms of general weakness. They gave their patients Vitamin A injections. The results were horrible. The flesh started rotting away from the hole caused by the injection. And in every case the victim died.

W. Burchett, 'Daily Express', 5 September 1945

Source E   Nagasaki

This photograph was taken from an American observation plane at 11 am on 9 August 1945. Ten kilometres below, Nagasaki is a blazing inferno. 40,000 are already dead and another 60,000 seriously injured.

Source F   Surrender

The enemy has begun to employ a new and most cruel bomb, the power of which to do damage is indeed incalculable, taking many innocent lives. This is the reason why we have ordered the surrender.

Emperor Hirohito, surrender address in a radio broadcast to the Japanese people, 15 August 1945

Source G

We were sure that Japan was winning. Soon it would be over. Our radio broadcasts told us of the glorious victories of our armies. We heard only good news of Japan. And we believed it. Thus it was a great shock to us when the newspapers and radio informed us that the war was moving closer and we Japanese must be prepared to fight on our own territory. We young girls could not believe what we heard. The history of our country went back 2,000 years. In all that time Japan had never been invaded. We had been taught that it never could be. Our country was protected by the gods. We were confident that we would win this war, as we had all others, because we were the country of the gods. We were sure the gods would send some miracle to protect us from the cruel Americans.

N. Hiroko, interviewed in 1984

Activities

1. Look at Sources A, B and C. Why do you think the Allies decided to drop atom bombs on Japan?

2. Use Sources D, E and F to explain why Japan surrendered.

3. Look at Sources B and G. What did the Japanese feel about surrender?

4. Do you think the Allies were justified in dropping atom bombs on Japan? Give reasons for your answer.

The Nuclear Age

After the Second World War nuclear technology continued to be developed. This was the era of the 'Cold War' between the two 'superpowers' (the USA and the Soviet Union) – a war of words and threats in which each side built up huge stockpiles of arms including nuclear weapons. Neither superpower wanted to be outdone by the other. One result of the Cold War is that nuclear weapons today are much more powerful than those dropped on Hiroshima and Nagasaki. They exist in numbers which could destroy the whole world several times over.

In 1946 British nuclear scientists who worked on the Manhattan Project returned from the USA. They began to develop nuclear power for generating electricity. The UK's first nuclear power stations began operation in 1956. Today they provide about 17% of the UK's electricity supply. Nuclear power was born out of the atom bomb project.

Source A   Nuclear energy – the case for and against

For – many countries use nuclear power stations (such as Sellafield above) to supply electricity because fossil fuels (coal, gas and oil) are becoming scarcer. Supporters see it as a clean source of energy because it produces little carbon dioxide (the main 'greenhouse' gas causing global warming).

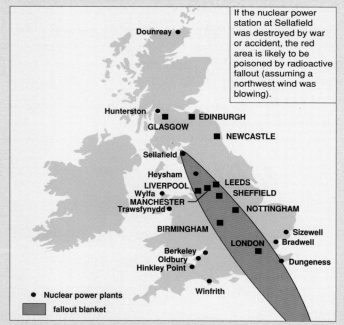

If the nuclear power station at Sellafield was destroyed by war or accident, the red area is likely to be poisoned by radioactive fallout (assuming a northwest wind was blowing).

- Nuclear power plants
- fallout blanket

Against – some people think that nuclear power stations are dangerous because of the risk of radiation leaks. Radiation can cause deadly diseases in animals and people and can poison crops and water supplies.

Source B   Nuclear weapons – the case for and against

For – some people think that having nuclear weapons acts as a 'deterrent'. It stops an enemy from attacking because they know a war would probably end up destroying the whole planet.

Against – others think that all nuclear weapons should be scrapped. It is too dangerous to have them around at all. This is the view of CND (Campaign for Nuclear Disarmament) pictured above.

Source C   Chernobyl

Decontaminating Chernobyl, May 1986

On 25 April 1986 the nuclear power station at Chernobyl in the Soviet Union exploded as a result of human error. 31 workers and firefighters died within days (of radiation burns) and 50,000 square kilometres of surrounding land was contaminated. The nuclear fallout reached 20 countries, including Britain. Scientists have estimated that between 280,000 and 500,000 deaths will result worldwide from this accident.

Greenpeace, 'Nuclear Power', 1992

Source D   Nuclear disarmament

Decommissioning nuclear weapons (making them harmless) in the former Soviet Union in line with the Soviet-American Treaty.

Although the Cold War is over, both the USA and Russia intend to keep large nuclear forces. It is estimated that by the year 2000 at least 6,000 nuclear weapons will remain on each side.

'The Guardian', July 1992

Source E   The spread of nuclear weapons

The United States invented nuclear weapons because it feared that Nazi Germany would build them first. The Soviet Union developed nuclear weapons to offset the American advantage. Britain and France built nuclear weapons to deter the Soviet Union. China's nuclear weapons were a response to American, and later Soviet, nuclear forces. India needs nuclear weapons because China invaded India in living memory. Pakistan needs nuclear weapons if India is going to have any. Israel needs nuclear weapons because of the threat of an Arab nuclear weapon. Israeli nuclear weapons prompt Arab nations to aim for nuclear capability.

C. Sagan and R. Turco, 'A Path Where No Man Thought', 1990

Checklist

- During the war there was a race to invent the atom bomb. Although Germany decided to drop out of the race, the Allies did not know this. The first atom bomb was exploded in a test in the USA in July 1945.

- In August 1945 atom bombs were dropped on Hiroshima and Nagasaki. This forced Japan to surrender.

- Today there are thousands of nuclear weapons and many countries use nuclear power to generate electricity.

Activities

1. Write an article about nuclear weapons for your local newspaper. Give the arguments for and against nuclear weapons and put your own point of view as a conclusion.

2. You are in charge of Britain's energy policy. Would you keep the existing nuclear power stations, build more or end nuclear power generation completely? Explain how you reached your answer.

3. 'The invention of the atom bomb was a turning point in the history of the world.' Use the sources on these pages to explain this statement.

9 THE POSTWAR WORLD

Central and Eastern Europe 1945

Berlin
GERMANY
POLAND
CZECHOSLOVAKIA
AUSTRIA
HUNGARY
YUGOSLAVIA
ROMANIA
ALBANIA
BULGARIA
GREECE
NORWAY
SWEDEN
FINLAND
SOVIET UNION
TURKEY
CYPRUS (British)
Mediterranean Sea
Suez Canal
LIBYA
EGYPT

— The iron curtain as defined by Churchill

Soviet Union

Territory gained by the Soviet Union since the start of World War II

Soviet occupation zones

Countries occupied by Soviet armies or with Communist governments after World War II

Themes

The wartime cooperation between Britain, the USA and the Soviet Union was shortlived. By the end of the 1940s Europe was split into the Communist East and the Capitalist West, each opposed to the other. Although there was a massive build up of arms, actual war did not break out in Europe. Hence the term Cold War. The Cold War lasted for nearly 45 years.

In 1945 many people hoped that conflicts would be solved by a new international organisation, the United Nations (UN). But the UN could only work effectively if the former wartime allies cooperated. As they began to quarrel, the problems of war-torn Europe increased. Economies had been badly damaged by the war and large numbers of people had been displaced from their homes.

This chapter looks at Europe after 1945 and asks these questions.

• Why did the wartime allies fall out?
• What happened to the millions of people displaced from their homes by the war?
• How successful was the new UN?

Focus Activities

1. Suppose you had been Stalin's interpreter at the meeting described in the Focus. Explain what happened and what you thought about it.

2. Look at the maps on this page and the Focus.
   a) What evidence is there to show that Churchill and Stalin kept to their agreement of October 1944?
   b) Why do you think Stalin considered Romania, Bulgaria, Hungary and Yugoslavia as important to the Soviet Union?
   c) Why did Churchill want to have influence in Greece?

3. What does the Focus tell us about the leadership style of Churchill and Stalin?

The Percentages Deal, 1944

After the Normandy landings in June 1944, the Germans were caught between the Soviet army in the east and the British and American armies in the west. Allied victory seemed inevitable. In October 1944 Churchill flew to Moscow to discuss the postwar settlement with Stalin. The USA wanted to postpone discussions about the postwar world until the war was over and so Roosevelt did not attend. Instead the USA sent an observer. But the observer was only present when Churchill and Stalin met in public. During a meeting held in private Churchill and Stalin made a secret deal about Europe – the 'Percentages Deal'. Whatever they said at later meetings, Churchill and Stalin both knew that eventually Europe would be divided into two parts – the Communist East and the Capitalist West.

Stalin was determined to keep control of the countries occupied by the Soviet Union during the war. In his view this meant making them into Communist countries. In 1944 he said, 'Whoever occupies a country also imposes on it his own system – it cannot be otherwise'.

Churchill realised that this was Stalin's view. His main concern was to safeguard British interests by making sure that certain countries remained outside the Communist bloc. The following passage was written by Churchill in his memoirs.

I said to Stalin, 'Let us settle our affairs in eastern Europe. Your armies are in Romania and Bulgaria. We British have interests there. Don't let us get at cross purposes in small ways. How would it do for you to have 90% influence in Romania and for us to have 90% influence in Greece?' While this was being translated, I wrote out on a sheet of paper:

Romania: Soviet Union 90%, the others 10%
Greece: Great Britain 90%, Soviet Union 10%
Yugoslavia: 50-50%
Hungary: 50-50%
Bulgaria: Soviet Union 75%, the others 25%.

I pushed this across to Stalin. He took his blue pencil and made a large tick on it and passed it back. It was all settled in no time. The paper lay in the middle of the table. I said, 'Might it not seem cynical (uncaring) if it seemed we had settled these issues, so important to so many millions of people, in such an offhand way? Let us burn the paper.' 'No, you keep it', he said.

Winston Churchill, 'Triumph and Tragedy', 1954

In 1946 Churchill spoke of an imaginary iron curtain descending across Europe. Joe refers to Joseph Stalin.

The boundaries in central and eastern Europe were fixed according to the position of the Allied armies at the end of the war – and stayed like this with very few changes until 1990.

Refugees

One result of total war was that vast numbers of people were uprooted from their homes and became refugees. For example, millions of French people fled their homes to escape the invading Germans in June 1940 and nine million foreign labourers were forced to go to Germany to work in German factories.

After 1945 changes of national boundaries (especially in eastern Europe) and the division of Europe into Communist and non Communist areas made the refugee problem greater. Large numbers of people were forcibly removed and resettled. For example, almost all Germans were expelled from Czechoslovakia and Hungary and over 400,000 Finns were driven out when the Soviet Union took over part of Finland.

Some people chose to move. Many Jews who had survived the Holocaust moved to their new homeland, Israel, which became a state on 14 May 1948.

Source A   Population movements 1945-49

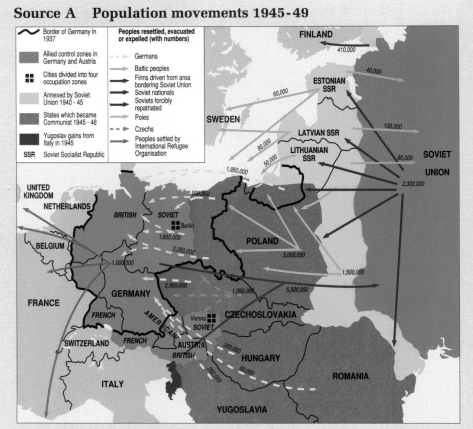

Key:
- Border of Germany in 1937
- Allied control zones in Germany and Austria
- Cities divided into four occupation zones
- Annexed by Soviet Union 1940 - 45
- States which became Communist 1945 - 48
- Yugoslav gains from Italy in 1945
- **SSR** Soviet Socialist Republic

Peoples resettled, evacuated or expelled (with numbers)
- Germans
- Baltic peoples
- Finns driven from area bordering Soviet Union
- Soviet nationals
- Soviets forcibly repatriated
- Poles
- Czechs
- Peoples settled by International Refugee Organisation

In 1945 Germany and Austria were divided into four occupation zones. Each zone was controlled by one of the four Allies – Britain, France, the USA and the Soviet Union. In the second half of 1945 there were millions of refugees in Europe. By 1946 three quarters of them had been sent home. This massive resettlement programme was organised by international organisations such as the Red Cross and the United Nations.

Source B   The size of the problem

German refugees in 1945

Europe had never seen so many refugees – the total number displaced during the war was 30 million or more. At the end of the war the largest group of displaced persons came from the Soviet Union – over 7.2 million Soviet labourers and prisoners of war had survived the ordeal of wartime Germany. Next came the French, with 2 million including 765,000 civilian workers; over 1.5 million Poles and 700,000 Italians. Among the refugees were all sorts – Nazi sympathisers, resistance workers, ex-SS, Communists, concentration camp guards, entire family groups, endless streams of people with pathetic bundles of belongings, usually in handcarts.

M. R. Marrus, 'Unwanted: European Refugees in the Twentieth Century', 1985

Source C Rehabilitation

The war in Europe was over. After the rejoicing came the reckoning. The International Red Cross began the work (that has lasted to the present day) of reuniting broken families. The refugees from Hitler's armament factories, mines and oil refineries – his slave labour force – were now adrift on a chaotic continent. Their homes were gone, the whereabouts of their families unknown. Referred to as 'Displaced Persons' (DPs), they were given food and shelter in temporary camps run by the Allied armies and the Red Cross. The DP camps became home for thousands of people. The young met and married there and eventually took a gamble together when a new life was offered in Australia or Canada. They put their past behind them. Many never saw their families again nor knew whether they were alive or not. But the survivors of the concentration camps presented a more difficult problem. Rehabilitation into a free world was going to be a slow process.

Brenda McBryde, a British nurse in Germany at the end of the war, 'A Nurse's War', 1986

Source F Fifty years later and still refugees

A great migration is underway in central Asia. The peoples whom Stalin punished by exile to Kazakhstan fifty years ago are going home. Millions of Germans, Greeks, Koreans and others are selling their homes and packing their bags. More than a million Germans were brought here in 1941 and suffered in the labour camps. Later they were released and their children intermarried and were educated only in Russian.

For many, such as Heinz Pfeffer, a retired professor of German, the choice of whether to stay or go is painful. 'My son married a Russian and their children only speak Russian and think of the Soviet Union as their home. But what can we do if we want to keep our identity?' He has applied to emigrate to Germany.

'The Times', 19 March 1992

Source D Going home

In the summer of 1945 Brenda McBryde worked in a hospital that had been set up to help the survivors of the concentration camps. She found that it was not just a matter of healing physical wounds.

By the end of July 1945 the condition of some of the patients had improved sufficiently for them to be transferred to a Displaced Persons' Camp as the next stage in rehabilitation. Here their background would be investigated and every effort made to reunite them with their families. Those on the transfer list, however, were thrown into utter dejection by the news. 'Soon you will be going home', we tried to explain. But 'home' was a word they had forgotten. Home was here in this familiar ward with us. At last they had learned to trust us. We were the only family they wanted to know about and they did not want to leave.

Brenda McBryde, 'A Nurse's War', 1986

Source E A Jewish homeland

Jewish refugees arriving in Palestine, April 1947

Many of the Jews who survived the Holocaust hoped to create a new homeland in Palestine. In 1948 the Jewish state of Israel was set up. Many Palestinian Arabs were driven out of their former country and became refugees.

Activities

1. Using Sources A and B explain why there were so many people moving around Europe after the war.

2. According to Sources C, D, E and F what was the refugee problem and how successfully was it overcome?

The United Nations

The Big Three had agreed at the Tehran Conference in 1943 to set up a new international organisation to replace the League of Nations. The United Nations was officially launched at the San Francisco conference in 1945. Representatives from fifty countries signed the United Nations Charter at this conference.

Source A The aims of the United Nations

We are determined to save succeeding generations from the scourge of war which twice in our lifetime has brought untold misery to mankind.

Article 1

To achieve international cooperation in solving international problems, to promote respect for human rights and fundamental freedoms for all without distinction as to race, sex, language or religion.

'United Nations Charter', June 1945

Source B Universal Declaration of Human Rights

Article 1

All human beings are born free and equal in dignity and rights. They are endowed with reason and conscience and should act towards one another in a spirit of brotherhood.

Article 2

Everyone is entitled to all the rights and freedoms set forth in this Declaration, without distinction of any kind, such as race, colour, sex, language, religion, political or other opinion, national or social origin, property, birth or other status.

Article 3

Everyone has the right to life, liberty and security of person.

Article 4

No one shall be held in slavery or servitude; slavery and the slave trade shall be prohibited in all their forms.

Article 5

No one shall be subjected to torture or to cruel, inhuman or degrading treatment or punishment.

United Nations, 'Universal Declaration of Human Rights', December 1948

Source C The United Nations

The Security Council

Members: 11 nations - 5 permanent members (the USA, the Soviet Union, Britain, France and China) and 6 countries elected every 2 years. Permanent members have the veto. This means they all have to agree before action is taken - any permanent member can block a decision by using its power of veto. From 1946 to 1964 the veto was used 103 times by the Soviet Union, 4 times by Britain, 3 times by France and once by China.

Function: to consider the recommendations of the General Assembly and to act on them (so long as they are not vetoed).

The General Assembly

Members: all member countries can send one representative to the General Assembly and have one vote each.

Function: to discuss all matters relating to the Charter and to make recommendations to the Security Council.

The Secretariat

Members: the Secretary General and staff. The Secretary General is appointed for 5 year terms. Six men (all from smaller countries) have held the post since 1945.

Function: to oversee the work of the UN. It must not take sides.

The Court of International Justice

Members: 15 judges elected for 9 year terms.

Function: to examine cases of international law. The court gives, on request, legal opinions on international disputes.

The Economic and Social Council

Members: the General Assembly elects members and the Council works through a series of agencies, for example:
UNESCO (United Nations Educational, Scientific and Cultural Organisation)
FAO (Food and Agricultural Organisation)
WHO (World Health Organisation)
ILO (International Labour Organisation)
UNICEF (United Nations International Children's Emergency Fund)

Source D

ONE WORLD
UN MONDE
ОДИН МИР

JOIN
UNITED NATIONS ASSOCIATION

Poster for the foundation of the UN in 1945

Source G   Relief agencies

UN food aid in Ethiopia. A blue wrist band is about to be attached to show the boy weighs less than 80% of his proper weight.

Source E   The Security Council and the veto

The power of the veto, highly valued by each of the permanent members, made the Security Council ineffective for taking action against the superpowers (the Soviet Union and the USA) and the United Nations became closely bound up with the Cold War.

D. Thomson, 'Europe Since Napoleon', 1957

The existence of the veto has often been criticised and its frequent use by the Soviet Union in the early days was condemned by the West. But no major nation can be forced to act against what it sees as its own interests.

E.G. Rayner, 'International Affairs', 1983

Source F   The UN as peacekeeper

Arab/Israeli conflict: From 1957 to 1967 a UN peacekeeping force stood between Israel and Egypt. Within weeks of the departure of the peacekeeping force the 1967 Arab/Israeli war broke out.

Korea (1950-53): UN forces (mainly from the USA but also from 15 other countries) were sent to drive back North Korean armies which had invaded South Korea.

Congo (1960): When the Congo (a Belgian colony in Africa) became independent in 1960, law and order quickly broke down. The UN sent in 20,000 troops (mainly from India, Ghana, Ireland, Canada and Nigeria) to restore order.

Activities

1. Look at Sources A, B, C and D. Briefly outline the main aims of the UN.

2. The introduction to the *Universal Declaration of Human Rights* (Source B) states, 'These rights belong to you. They are your rights. Help to promote and defend them for yourself as well as for your fellow human beings.'

   a) Do you think this statement is a good idea? Explain your answer.

   b) How might you help to 'promote and defend' these rights?

   c) What difficulties might there be in putting the Declaration into practice?

3. Look at Sources C and E. Why was it difficult for the UN to act against the superpowers?

4. What evidence do Sources F and G provide to show that the UN is an *international* organisation?

The Cold War

The Cold War has been described as, 'a state of extreme tension between the superpowers, stopping short of all out war'. The superpowers were the USA and the Soviet Union. The first 'battles' of the Cold War were fought in Germany because that is where the armies of the wartime Allies met. Germany remained divided until 1990. The division of Germany became a symbol of the division of postwar Europe.

Source B   Churchill and Stalin 1946

All the ancient states of central and eastern Europe lie in the Soviet sphere and are subject to control from Moscow. The Soviet Union wishes to extend its power indefinitely.

Churchill's 'Iron Curtain' speech, March 1946

In 1941 the Germans invaded the Soviet Union through Poland, Romania, Bulgaria and Hungary because these countries had governments hostile to the Soviet Union. Is it surprising that we should want to see governments friendly to the Soviet Union in these countries?

Stalin, 'Pravda' (a Soviet newspaper), March 1946

Source C   Germany – the meeting point

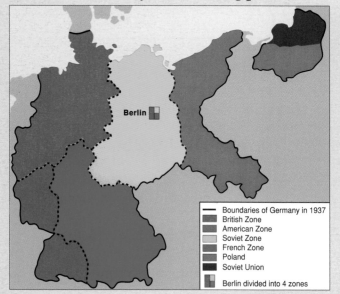

	Boundaries of Germany in 1937
	British Zone
	American Zone
	Soviet Zone
	French Zone
	Poland
	Soviet Union
	Berlin divided into 4 zones

At the end of the war the three wartime Allies and France agreed to divide Germany into four zones until they decided its future. Berlin was also divided into four. As the former Allies began to quarrel, so Germany remained divided.

Source A   Causes of conflict

A Soviet view of the USA. The flags represent American military bases. The man in the soldier's back pocket is an American politician. He is holding an olive branch and shouting peace slogans. The Cold War was in part a contest between two different systems – Capitalism in the West and Communism in the East. In Capitalist countries, industry is privately owned whilst in Communist countries industry is state owned. The Cold War was also a result of fear and misunderstanding on both sides.

An American view of the Soviet Union. The Soviet Union is represented by a bear.

Source D   The Berlin crisis 1948-49

The possibility of a reunited Germany frightened the Soviet Union. In 1948, fearing that the West intended to unite its zones in Germany, the Soviets closed down the road, rail and canal routes through their zone to Berlin. The 2 million people in West Berlin (the parts occupied by Britain, the USA and France) relied on the West for food, fuel and clothing. For the next 11 months the Berlin airlift (277,728 flights from the West) supplied West Berlin until the Soviet blockade ended. In 1949 the 3 western zones were united to form the Federal German Republic – West Germany. The eastern zone became the German Democratic Republic (East Germany), a Communist state.

Source G   Communism overturned

Statue of Lenin dismantled in Lithuania, 23 August 1991. Formerly part of the Soviet Union, Lithuania has now banned the Communist Party.

Source E   The Berlin wall

Berlin continued to be the symbol of tension in the Cold War. In 1961 the Communist East German government built a wall to stop its people from escaping to the West and to prevent contact between people in the east and west of the city. In 1989 the wall was pulled down. In 1990 West and East Germany were reunified. This picture shows the Berlin wall in 1989.

Source F   The end of the Cold War

The attempts by President Mikhail Gorbachev to reform the Soviet system led finally to the collapse of Soviet Communism in 1991. The Cold War was over. The Soviet Union broke up into 15 separate nations and Communist governments were overthrown in the eastern European countries formerly under Soviet control. This picture shows Boris Yeltsin sworn in as President of the new Russian Republic, 10 July 1991.

Activities

1. What do Sources A and B tell us about the causes of the Cold War?
2. Using Sources C, D and E explain why Berlin became a 'symbol' both of the Cold War and the end of the Cold War.
3. 'A new Cold War between superpowers is unlikely.' Explain this statement using Sources F and G.

Checklist

- Postwar Europe was split between the Capitalist West and the Communist East.
- At the end of the Second World War there were over 30 million refugees.
- The United Nations was created in 1945.
- Communism collapsed in 1990-91. The Cold War was over.

Acknowledgements

Cover design   Caroline Waring-Collins (Waring Collins Partnership)

Illustrations   Caroline Waring-Collins (Waring Collins Partnership)

Page design   Andrew Allen

Reader   Lisa Fabry

Picture credits

Brick 7 (all); Bridgeman Art Library/Roy Miles Fine Paintings, London 39 (b); CND 86 (bl); Daily Express 81 (t); Fondazione Biblioteca Archivio Luigi Micheletti 17; Kate Haralambos 15 (mr); Hulton Deutsch 6 (r), 8 (bl), 11 (t), 15 (ml), 23 (m), 31 (r), 35 (r), 36 (t), 37 (m), 39 (t), 40 (t), 64 (tr); Imperial War Museum 41 (t and m), 42 (m), 43 (ml), 47 (t and m), 48 (l), 73, 74 (t); Mansell Collection 15 (t); Mary Evans Picture Library 9 (t), 22; Novosti 6 (l), 10, 27, 48 (r), 51 (t), 65 (tl), 71 (mr); Peter Newark's Historical Pictures 14 (t and b), 16 (br), 25 (br), 26 (r), 43 (t), 44 (t), 46 (t), 55 (m), 56 (t), 62 (m), 64 (br), 68 (b), 70 (br), 75; Picturepoint 4 (b), 26 (l), 28 (r), 29 (l), 38 (t), 59, 72 (l), 86 (tr); Popperfoto 18 (m), 20 (t), 20 (b), 23 (l), 25 (bl), 35 (l), 38 (b), 45 (tr), 71 (ml), 81 (b), 90, 91, 95 (bl); Rex Features 69 (br); Robert Hunt Library 20 (m), 53 (tl), 63 (tl), 68 (m), 79; SCR 8 (br), 9 (b), 52 (mr), 66 (tr), 67 (t), 87 (m); Times Books 4 (m) Reproduced from 'The Times Concise Atlas of World History' by kind permission; Topham Picture Source 18 (t), 24 (r), 37 (t), 49, 50 (bl), 52 (bl), 54 (t), 57, 58 (br), 62 (l), 64 (tl), 66 (br), 69 (tl), 80, 83 (t), 84 (t), 86 (tl), 87 (t), 92, 93 (t), 95 (tl, tr and br); UNICEF 93 (b); Vintage Magazine Co 42 (b); Weidenfeld Archive 5, 29 (r), 64 (br); Weimar Archive 24 (tl), 25 (tr), 82 (l); Wiener Library/ The Beate Klanfeld Foundation 76; Weiner Library/'People' 72 (r).

Every effort has been made to locate the copyright owners of material used in this book. Any omissions brought to our attention are regretted and will be credited in subsequent printings.

Causeway Press Ltd
PO Box 13, Ormskirk, Lancashire L39 5HP

© Tony Lancaster, Steve Lancaster, Lisa Fabry 1993

1st impression 1993

British Library Cataloguing in Publication Data - a catalogue record for this book is available from the British Library.

ISBN 0 946183 98 8

Typesetting by John A. Collins, (Waring Collins Partnership), Ormskirk, Lancashire L39 1QR
Printed and bound by Cambus Litho Ltd, East Kilbride